"Hearing God's Call: Step Into your Purpose and Destiny

MISHAWN CHILDERS

The Voice
Copyright © 2025 Mishawn Childers

All rights reserved. This is a fiction book. Any resemblance to any persons dead or alive is purely coincidental. No part of this book can be replicated or duplicated without reference to the book. No part of this book may be stored in a retrieval system, database, and or published in any form or by any means, electronic, mechanical, photocopying, recording, or otherwise, without the prior written permission of the author and or publisher.

ISBN: 979-8-218-44397-9

Speaker, Author & Life Coach
Mishawn Childers
www.mishawnchilders.com

Editing by:
Jhordynn
www.jhordynn.com

Editing & Formatting by:
Lorraine Reguly from
www.WordingWell.com

Cover & Interior Design by:
Carlos V. Kaigler/ C'vaughn'K Graphic Designs/ Author The Poet B.GKL
www.authorbgkl.com

"I hope that the stories in this book encourage and inspire you to walk in faith and listen to, The Voice."

WHY I WROTE THIS BOOK

I wrote **The Voice** because I know what it feels like to be trapped—trapped by self-doubt, fear, past wounds, and the feeling that you're not enough. I know what it's like to wonder if God is speaking, to question if I have a greater purpose, and to feel like I'll never break free from the cycle of comparison and uncertainty.

But I also know what it's like to **hear God's call**—to step out in faith, embrace my destiny, and walk in the abundant life He designed for me. And I want the same for you.

This book is for every woman who is **tired of being stuck** and **ready to move forward.** It's for the woman who longs to hear God's voice clearly, step into her purpose with confidence, and finally live the life He created her for.

If you're reading this, **it's not by accident.** God is calling you higher. This book is your invitation to listen, trust, and step boldly into the destiny waiting for you.

WHO THIS BOOK IS FOR

This book is for you if:

- You struggle with **self-doubt, fear, and limiting beliefs** that keep you from moving forward.
- You feel **stuck in past pain, uncertainty, or comparison**, wondering if God has more for you.
- You long to **hear God's voice clearly** and understand the purpose He has for your life.
- You're ready to **break free from old patterns, embrace change, and step into your destiny** with boldness.
- You desire to **build a life and business** that aligns with God's calling and brings true fulfillment.

Whether you're navigating personal struggles, stepping into a new season, or leading others, this book will equip you with the faith, clarity, and courage to **step into the life God designed for you.**

HOW TO READ THIS BOOK

The Voice is more than just a book—it's a **journey** toward transformation. Each chapter is designed to help you hear God's voice, overcome obstacles, and step confidently into your destiny.

To get the most out of this experience:

☑ **Use the Journal & Workbook:** This book comes with a **companion journal and workbook** to help you dive deeper into self-reflection, prayer, and action. These tools are designed to guide you step by step through this journey. You can purchase them at **[insert website or purchase details]**.

☑ **Read with a Group or Training Setting: The Voice** is powerful on its own, but it's even more transformative when read in a **group setting.** Whether you're in a Bible study, mentorship group, or leading a women's ministry, this book can be used for **group discussions and training sessions.** Each chapter includes **reflection questions and action steps** to help you apply what you've learned.

☑ **Take Your Time & Take Action:** This book isn't meant to be skimmed—it's meant to be **lived.** Take time to **pray, reflect, and apply** what you read. The more you engage with it, the more transformation you'll see in your life.

Dedication

*T*o my **amazing husband, James**,
Your unwavering love, support, and belief in me have been my foundation. Thank you for walking this journey of faith with me. I am beyond blessed to have you by my side.

To my incredible children, **Alexis, Jalyn, Justus, and London**,
You are my greatest joy and my greatest inspiration. Your strength, resilience, and love remind me every day of God's goodness. I pray that you always walk boldly in the purpose He has for you.

To my **dear friends and family**,
Your encouragement, prayers, and presence in my life have meant more than words can express. Thank you for believing in me, uplifting me, and reminding me that I am never alone.

With love and gratitude,
Mishawn Childers

Table of Contents

Part 1- Stagnation

Chapter 1: The Signs 4
Chapter 2: Self- Love 10
Chapter 3: Missed Blessings 17
Chapter 4 My Brother 26
Chapter 5: Hidden Enemies 37
Chapter 6 The Whisper 43

Part 2- Transformation

Chapter 7: Moving On 51
Chapter 8: The Present 57
Conclusion: As the Voice Guides You… 67
    The Voice Oath 69
    Trust Your Inner Guide to Discover the Wisdom Within: A Workbook to Assist You 70
    The Voice is Your Superpower but How Do You Know It's His Voice? 73
    Embrace Your Superpower 76
    Navigating Confusion: When Your Feelings Conflict with the Voice of the Divine Creator 77
    The Importance of Acting on the Voice 80
    Personal Guide to Hearing the Voice of the Divine Creator 84
    Final Reflection and Commitment 85
    A Note from the Author 89
About The Author 90

A Note To The Reader

In some of the following stories, the Bible is quoted. All quotes come from the King James Version. I hope you enjoy the stories, and that they "speak" to you. When you listen to and obey **_The Voice_** of the Divine Creator, you will be rewarded, and your greatest potential will be achieved.

Throughout this book, I use the term 'Divine Creator' to refer to the higher power that guides and connects us. For some, this will mean God; for others, it may reflect a different understanding of the divine. Additionally, I often reference the concept of the Holy Spirit or 'The Voice' which represents the still, small voice that leads us with wisdom and clarity. My intention is to make this book accessible to everyone, regardless of their spiritual or religious background, while honoring the universal truths and divine guidance that unite us all.

The Voice Workbook

Your journey to hearing the Voice of the Divine Creator doesn't end here. Dive deeper with The Voice Workbook, where you'll uncover and remove the mindset blocks, self-doubt, and limiting beliefs that can cloud your connection and purpose. Let the Voice guide you fully—inside and out.

"Always aspire to reach higher."

"Surely the Divine Creator will do nothing, but he revealeth his secret unto his servants the prophets." **(Amos 3:7, KJV)**

Chapter 1: The Signs

Dealing with Abuse and Ignoring the Signs....

"Mr. and Mrs. Phoenix, it was so nice meeting you. I had a great time tonight. The food was delicious," their daughter Kaia's boyfriend, Cain, said. Turning his head, Cain grinned at Kaia's dad, "I'm sorry I had to beat you like that in Spades, but competing is in my DNA." "It was nice to meet you, too, Cain," responded Mr. Phoenix.

"We will have to schedule another game night soon. I am still a little rusty, but I'll leave you crying next time." "Excuses, excuses." Cain jokingly rolled his eyes.

"Next time, I'll beat you again." "You're probably right," Mr. Phoenix replied, laughing. Cain and Kaia walked slowly toward the moonlight that was dancing on the porch and decided to sit outside and chat for a bit. "Kaia, I had such a great time with you and your family. You all are amazing. I've been thinking about us, a lot."

He grabbed her hand in the still darkness of the night and continued talking. "I want to focus on building a future together. What do you think about that?" Kaia was excited by the thought of having a serious relationship with such a seemingly good man. She smiled, grabbed his hand, and held it tightly, whispering softly, "I would love that." Sitting quietly in the moonlight's glow, staring into his eyes and getting lost in the moment, she suddenly had a peculiar feeling that she had never felt before. It was as though her gut turned into a knot, warning her of impending doom. She quickly turned it off, but not fast enough. Cain looked at her quizzically as he noticed her split-second apprehension.

"What?" he asked her. "Why did you tense up?" "Your eyes. It's something about your eyes…" Kaia had no idea what it was about Cain's eyes. But something about them told her to run away and never

THE VOICE: MISHAWN CHILDERS

look back. An internal voice, a gut feeling, her intuition—something. But she didn't listen. That voice told her to leave him alone, but she couldn't give herself a good reason to walk away.

He didn't talk to her crazy-like, steal from her, or abuse her in any way. He was a regular guy. There was nothing extraordinary about him, but nothing alarming about him, either. He spoke up. "I'm not mixed. Everybody always asks me that.

My eyes are green because of the French Creoles, way deep down the family line. They're from Louisiana. But at the end of the day, my mama is Black; my daddy is Black, and I'm Black, too." Kaia nodded her head, but that wasn't it. Even though his eyes were a light olive green, there was a darkness to them that she couldn't ignore. But she continued to put it in the back of her mind because this young man had done nothing to her.

Kaia, a beautiful, carefree, and outspoken sixteen-year-old girl, was growing up quickly in West Texas. Everywhere she went, she had an air of curiosity mixed with a bit of skepticism, as rose-colored glasses had never served her well. She saw life and situations for what they were. She never sugar-coated anything. She never saw the glass as half full nor half empty; she saw that the glass needed to be refilled.

Her brothers John, Jr. and William were athletic, agreeable, and mild-mannered, but that was not Kaia's nature at all. She was fiery and passionate. She would argue just for the sake of arguing. Although she spoke very frankly about many things, she lacked confidence, which caused her to hide behind biased opinions without many facts to back them up. So, when Cain's eyes kept getting her attention, she kept writing it off as her paranoia. But the thoughts kept creeping back in, and The Voice kept alerting her. *What is it about his eyes?*

Six uneventful years of off-and-on dating went by. It was like a typical teen drama: break up to make up. They spent a few years apart and made their way back to each other when Kaia was twenty-two. She made her mind up that she was now ready to grow up and be *for real* about their relationship this time. No more breaking up because he didn't fall asleep on the phone with her, and he agreed to always fall asleep on the phone with her. No more walking away because he forgot the onions on her burger, and he agreed to always order onions for her burger. No more petty, high school foolishness. She was now a young woman and decided that it was time to start acting like it.

Cain knew that he was now a young man, so it was time for him to act like it. He decided that he wasn't going to break up with her just because she talked loudly when the game was on, and she agreed to not talk loudly when the game was on. He said that he wasn't going to leave her if she took too long to call him back, and she agreed to always call him back within a reasonable amount of time.

Life had matured them both. They were ready to move towards "marriage and forever." The childish things had to end. No matter how much they matured, changed, and forgave each other, The Voice continued to give Kaia the same warning He had given her when she was sixteen years young: *Leave Cain alone*. She ignored The Voice, wrote it off as her typical paranoia, and continued to "do life" with Cain.

One thing that Cain expressed to Kaia that he didn't like was that she wasn't spontaneous enough; he could guess her every move.

He knew what she was going to do, what time she was going to do it, how long she was going to do it, and when she would do it again. As part of working on herself in their relationship, Kaia aimed to change that. Every day at two p.m., she went to a coffee shop to study. This day, she decided to surprise Cain and pop up at his house, unannounced. This was her being spontaneous and unpredictable, as he had requested. She had a key to his apartment, so she walked right on in, and there Cain and another woman were, on his couch, screaming the Divine Creator's name, without a Bible in sight. Kaia was so blinded by rage that she couldn't say anything to either one of them. She knew that if she reacted, she'd go to prison. She swallowed her fury and rushed to his room to pack her things and go.

Cain chased Kaia into the bedroom, spitting out a whole bunch of lies and expletives. He flipped it to make it seem as if everything was Kaia's fault. The one-sided conversation went from him saying, "It's not what it looks like" to, "Had you told me you were on your way, I could have saved you from this" to, "Since your head is always in a book, I had to get attention from somewhere!"

Kaia simply kept quiet, tamping down her anger. She made a conscious decision not to outwardly react and continued packing whatever she could fit inside her purse. But then he grabbed her wrist to stop her from packing, and the atmosphere changed.

Out of exasperation, frustration, and all kinds of other negative emotions pulsating through Kaia, she threw a shirt across the room to keep from putting her hands on him. That action triggered something in Cain that he had buried deep inside of him. His eyes clouded over. He pulled a gun out of a dresser drawer and placed it at Kaia's temple. "Cain, what are you doing?

Oh, my Divine Creator! Put the gun down!" Cain stood, consumed with anger. His eyes were dark and crazed as if possessed by an evil spirit full of rage. He pointed the gun directly at Kaia's face and aimed it between her eyes. Kaia gripped with fear and panic, could not believe that the man she once cared deeply for could flip a mental switch like that.

A million thoughts raced in her mind. *What if he kills me? Should I just run away? How did I not see this side of him? Were the signs there all along, and I just ignored them? Is this what The Voice was warning me about?* His eyes held her captive and wouldn't let her go. They were dark and blank, soul-less, lifeless, reckless. And there it was. That is what she saw when she was sixteen years young, but she just didn't recognize it. She saw the devil in his eyes.

"My parents threw stuff across the room all the time before they beat me. You think I'm gonna let you beat me? You think I'm gonna let you make me less of a man? You think you're gonna have that power over me? Bow down! I run this show!" Cain shouted at Kaia. As afraid for her life as Kaia was, she knew one thing for certain: she would not bow down to anyone, except the Divine Creator.

THE VOICE: MISHAWN CHILDERS

The Divine Creator had tried to warn her to walk away when she was sixteen when his eyes spoke to her, but she didn't listen. She was listening now. She boldly walked away from the gun pointed between her eyes. On her way out, she walked past the woman sitting on the couch. The woman didn't say or do anything. She never moved.

Years later, Kaia found out that he physically abused that woman and plenty of other women. Thankfully, she got out before her name was added to the list. She vowed that the last time that she looked into his eyes would be the last time. There was *always* something about his eyes…

THE VOICE: MISHAWN CHILDERS

"The eye is the lamp of the body. If your eyes are healthy, your whole body will be full of light. 23 But if your eyes are unhealthy, your whole body will be full of darkness." **(Matthew 6:22-23, KJV)**

Chapter 2: Self- Love

Stop Comparing Yourself to Others

"I don't know. I don't think that it is supposed to hurt this bad," Denise whimpered to her friend Marcy. "I know I just had the surgery yesterday, but it feels like something is off." Denise and Marcy were both on their knees, in a praying position, flying back to the United States from Mexico. They had each just gotten a Brazilian butt lift (BBL) the day before, so they weren't allowed to sit on their buttocks yet.

The entire plane was filled with men and women flying back to the United States on their knees because they had just gotten BBLs as well. "Surgery hurts, Denise. Quit whining like a baby," Marcy told her. "I know surgery hurts. I've had surgery before but look at everybody else. They probably had surgery yesterday, too, and they are laughing.

You couldn't pay me to laugh right now, and I am taking pain pills around the clock. Even you aren't in as much pain as I am. And I know for certain you had surgery yesterday, just like I did. We were in the same office at the same time." "Everybody deals with pain differently.

You can't compare yourself to others. Suck it up, buttercup. You've already had the surgery. In a few weeks, once everything settles, you are going to be looking fine! We will get all the men. Thomas is going to hate that he turned you down. He is about to eat your dust."

Marcy grinned. Denise tried to keep an open, optimistic mind, but the throbbing pain and burning in her thighs and butt just wouldn't let her. The thought of Thomas crawling to her and begging to be with her put a smile on her face, but it wasn't enough to take away the agony she felt. "You went in with a negative attitude. That's why you're not healing well," Marcy told Denise. "All the 'I don't think I should do it. There's a voice telling me not to do it. Maybe I should cancel' that you were saying," Marcy mocked Denise.

"You were too negative, and you put that negativity out into the atmosphere. You manifested pain and poor healing." "I didn't manifest anything. I just told you what a voice kept telling me. It kept telling me to not get the surgery. But I did it anyway." The turbulence that was probably not a big deal for everyone else on the plane caused what felt like knives severing Denise's flesh from her bones.

What was a normal descent for all the other passengers caused what felt like a balloon popping inside Denise's abdomen and thighs. The usual bump of the tires hitting the pavement during the landing caused Denise's insides to drop into oblivion.

When Denise got off of her knees to get her luggage out of the stowaway compartment, Marcy immediately wrapped Denise's body with a blanket. Denise's clothes were drenched in blood, and Marcy didn't want anyone to see it.

"I *knew* I should have listened to that voice," Denise said, once she discovered that she was bleeding. Denise stripped down in the airport's bathroom to wash up and change clothes. What body parts she could touch and see were extremely bruised, swollen, and hardened. Finally, the bleeding stopped. "Can I see your body, Marcy? I know we're not supposed to compare, but I just want to see."

Marcy entered the handicapped stall with her friend and showed Denise her naked body. Denise immediately noticed that Marcy's body wasn't as swollen or bruised as hers. Marcy's body was already looking like the desired result. Yes, Marcy had some healing to do, but it was obvious that she was getting what she paid for. Denise rubbed different parts of Marcy's body.

Marcy's body was firm. Denise's body was hard. That was a big difference. "Let's just go home and give things time to settle. You start getting your lymphatic drainage massage next week. That will help with all this bruising, swelling, pain, and hardness," Marcy suggested to Denise.

"The more that time goes by, the more pain I'm in." "I saw you taking the pain pills. Maybe double the dosage?" "I'm not supposed to have to double the dosage. I don't even know if that's safe. I just should have listened to the voice." "Well, we're back in America now, Denise. What are you gonna do? Fly back to Mexico?" "I guess not. I barely have enough money to order off the dollar menu.

This flight and surgery took everything I got." Denise paused, and then added, "Okay. I will take another pain pill. I probably just need to sleep this off." Eight days passed, and Denise was in so much pain that she was screaming and panting. She was constantly sweating, and she could barely move.

Her skin felt like bricks, was as hot as a grease fire, and she was as purple as a grape. She had absolutely no money to go to an ER and get checked. Even if she had the money, she was too embarrassed to go. She didn't want anyone to know that she had had a BBL, let alone that she had gone to Mexico to get it done cheaply.

She had convinced herself that she just needed to get the lymphatic drainage massage, and she would be healed. Unlike Denise, Marcy was already back at work. But Denise remembered what her surgeon repeatedly told her: "You cannot compare your healing journey to anyone else's." Before getting the BBL, Denise prepaid for ten lymphatic drainage massages.

The first session was scheduled for Day Ten, post-op. She was so excited that Day Ten had finally arrived that she had forgotten that she could no longer walk unassisted. The pain and hardness in her buttocks wouldn't allow her to move like she used to. She used a walker to get into the car. Marcy drove her to the appointment.

On Day Ten, Denise's body felt like a boulder, and her purple bruises had turned black. Her sweating was a constant downpour, and she was having a few hallucinations. She was convinced that she was in need of a lymphatic drainage massage and figured that the massage would be the cure.

THE VOICE: MISHAWN CHILDERS

"You say that you can barely move your legs, Ms. Harrison?" the lymphatic massage drainage nurse asked Denise, concerned. "Yes. My butt hurts so badly that it's paralyzing me." Denise's voice was barely above a whisper. The side effects of this surgery were making her fade away, little by little. "I think you should see a doctor in the ER, not us. And you are sweating so badly," the nurse continued. "I know I need this massage because this morning, I started leaking fluid out of my butt cheek." "Okay. I am going to check your vitals." The nurse checked Denise's vital signs. "One hundred and two point five is your temperature.

Your blood pressure is low, and your pulse is high. Ms. Harrison, you have a very high fever, which is more than likely, the cause of your sweating and hallucinations. Your vital signs also indicate a severe infection. I'm going to call nine-one-one." "No. Just give me the massage," Denise whispered with what strength she had left. "No, Ma'am, but can you undress? I want to see this leaking you were talking about."

The nurse helped Denise take her dress off. "My Divine Creator!" the nurse exclaimed, as she looked at the black bruises on Denise's thighs, hips, and buttocks. She rubbed her hand across Denise's disfigured and deformed body and was mortified. "Ms. Harrison. You *need* to go to the ER. That is not up for debate. Where's the leakage?" Denise told her, "If you press down on my right butt cheek, you'll see it come out." The nurse pressed Denise's right butt cheek and observed what came out.

"This isn't fluid. This isn't liquid at all. This is... wet cement." The nurse rubbed the matter between her fingers to inspect and be sure. "You have to go to the hospital right now!" The nurse called 911 and informed Marcy—who was waiting in the lobby—of what was going on, with Denise's permission. Marcy ran into the room and hugged Denise. "I am so sorry. So, so sorry. I should have listened to you." "And I should have listened to the voice." Marcy was confused and said, "My surgeon didn't put cement in me... I don't think. And you were the only one on that plane in pain. What happened? Why did he do this?" Denise shook her head in defeat.

THE VOICE: MISHAWN CHILDERS

She had no idea. She had no answers for Marcy. "I know we had different surgeons, but we were at the same practice, at the same time. This doesn't make sense."

"Once you're outside of America, you are playing a game of Russian Roulette," the nurse said. "You would be surprised how easy it is to pose as a doctor in some of these countries, even if you never graduated middle school. All the hoops and velvet ropes and red tape that America makes doctors jump through don't even exist in other countries. All you have to do is show up in a white lab coat with fancy lingo, and you get the job."

"But the doctor who did this to Denise had to know he would get caught. He had to know that she wouldn't heal and would come back to sue him or something!" "Once again, most of these fake doctors are extremely uneducated and extremely poor. They perform about six surgeries in two to three days, collect those tens of thousands of dollars, then quit and disappear. It may have gotten them only thirty thousand dollars, but that is the most money they have ever seen. To them, they are rich.

Their goal is to be a thousandaire, and they get it by doing this. They're usually living in underdeveloped countries, in underdeveloped towns. They don't care. They just don't. Google it. People have been injected with antifreeze, tire sealant, cooking oil, and hand sanitizer. The list goes on. You are not the only one, Ms. Harrison. And you won't be the last.

Simply put, these fraudulent doctors have nothing to lose, and innocent lives mean nothing to them." The paramedics arrived and placed Denise on a stretcher. Denise was in and out of it after that, but she kept hearing them say, "She is such a pretty girl.

Why did she do this to herself?" That reminded her of the voice that kept telling her, *"Don't do this. Do not get this surgery. You are fearfully and wonderfully made. You were made in the Divine Creator's image. There's no need to fix what the Divine Creator put his paintbrush on."*

THE VOICE: MISHAWN CHILDERS

"Ms. Harrison," a doctor said to her, once she awakened from surgery. "I am Doctor Neil." Denise's fever was down, and she understood everything that he was saying. She just couldn't take it all in. It was too much. He basically told her that because the doctor destroyed her so badly by sucking out muscle along with fat and tissue, a lot of the cement had to be left in her body.

At that present time, there was no known way to safely remove the cement that would still allow her to live. It was an event that had not yet been studied. However, with her permission and with her signing a waiver, they would experiment with a lot of procedures on her to see what would restore her to a normal life and a normal look—if that was even possible.

Denise needed time to think about how she wanted to live the rest of her life. But she knew that having a permanent IV in her arm with a constant antibiotic dripping, being unable to move, and having a body badly warped wasn't it.

She knew that having to take pain medications every three hours and dealing with their side effects wasn't it. She knew that lying in a hospital bed until they found the cure wasn't it, either. Whatever she decided, she couldn't afford it. She couldn't afford to live, and she couldn't afford to die. If only she'd listened to The Voice.

"Yet ye have not hearkened unto me, saith the Divine Creator; that ye might provoke me to anger with the works of your hands to your hurt." **(Jeremiah 25:7, KJV)**

… THE VOICE: MISHAWN CHILDERS

Chapter 3: Missed Blessings

The Cost of Ignoring God's Voice

"I love Pizza Day!" Charity told her friends at the lunch table, holding a slice in her hand. "My mom says that I better eat all the pizza that I can now before they go to my thighs when I get to be her age. Blah, blah, blah," Charity said, as she took a large bite and then devoured the pizza.

Her friend, Octavia, chimed in. "Last night, my mom told me to stop chasing people. Like, Girl, I'm not trying to be old and lonely like you. She's in her thirties and only has *three* friends. Girl, you want me to be like you? No, thanks! I don't care that Ashley only talks to me when her other friends aren't around. Having somebody is better than having nobody. I don't care how fake they are."

The other four girls at the lunch table agreed. "Don't get me started on my dad with his Ted Talks. This morning" Charity's words stopped in her throat when she saw Brittany walk into the lunchroom. "Tell her what I told you last night," The Voice said to Charity. "What were you going to tell us about this morning with your dad, Charity?" Lindsey asked. "He… He… Um…" "Tell her what I told you to tell her," The Voice demanded. "Are you okay, Charity?" Grace asked her. "Yes. I'll be right back. I have to go tell Brittany something."

"Brittany? The cheerleader, Brittany?" Lindsey queried. Charity nodded her head as she stood. "She acts like she doesn't know you and hasn't spoken to you since elementary school. What in the world do yall have to talk about?" Grace asked her. Charity ignored Grace and began walking towards Brittany. Erica stopped Charity after only a few steps. "Girl, we don't associate ourselves with her.

We are better than her and her whole clique. And they think that they are better than us. Not to mention, her grades are so bad that she can't even cheer for the next six weeks. Girl, she is so not on our level. Stop! What are you doing?" Erica asked Charity.

"I can't explain it," Charity began. "There's like this voice inside my… body… that warns me about stuff and things like that. Every time I've listened to it, it was right. Whenever I didn't listen to it, bad things happened." "Voices? Do you need medicine? Like my uncle who hears voices?" Octavia asked. Her four friends began looking at Charity strangely. "No! Like, it's the Divine Creator or something," Charity answered. "You are only seventeen, Charity.

The Divine Creator doesn't talk to you," Grace said. Charity shook her head and kept walking towards Brittany. Charity had told herself the same thing: she was too young for the Divine Creator to talk to her. She had been telling herself that since she was eight years old. But she knew that it was *something, somebody*. And she knew that she wasn't schizophrenic.

That Voice had to be the Divine Creator. Had to be. "Hey, Brittany. Hey, guys," Charity spoke to Brittany and her friends, after swallowing her vomit. "Brittany, can I talk to you, please?" Brittany and her clique looked at each other in confusion. "Who are you?" Brittany laughed. "Do you even go here? Stranger danger!" Brittany and her clique laughed. Charity kept a solemn face. "Sure," Brittany finally relented, after realizing that Charity wasn't laughing or walking away. "Okay. Come here."

Charity walked into a corner of the lunchroom, and Brittany followed her. "I'm not sure if you remember me, but my name is Charity and we went to elementary school together. I'm a senior at this school, like you." "I don't remember you."

"That's fine. I know I'm gonna sound crazy, but there's this… voice… that keeps telling me to tell you to not go to a party tonight because if you do, something bad will happen." Brittany stared at Charity in silence for a few seconds before laughing in her face. "This… 'voice'… told you to tell me this, when I barely know who you are?" Brittany was incredulous. "I think you're just jealous because I was invited to the party, and you weren't."

THE VOICE: MISHAWN CHILDERS

The cheerleader crossed her arms in defiance. "I don't know what party you're talking about. I don't even know what party The Voice was talking about. I'm just telling you what the Divine Creator told me to tell you." "Is it a voice, or is it the Divine Creator? Make up your mind."

"I don't know, Brittany, okay? Just don't go. This... voice... is always right." "And what bad thing is going to happen if I do go?" "It didn't tell me. I don't know." "Let me get this right. This... voice... Divine Creator ... told you to warn me, but it didn't give you the whole story?" "Maybe the whole story isn't my business." "Yeah... You're jealous.

You claim you don't know about the party tonight, but who doesn't know about Lorenzo's Spring Break Bash? You know about it. You're just not invited. And you aren't about to scare me out of going." "Brit—" "Goodbye, Chasity, and Chasity's... voice." "It's *Charity*, not Chasity." "Potato, po-tah-toe." Brittany walked away, and Charity walked back to her friends at their lunch table. "What did you say to her? What did she say to you?" Grace asked Charity.

"I told her what the Divine Creator told me to tell her... to not go to a party tonight, or else something bad will happen. She pretty much laughed and walked away." "Well, I need you to ask the Divine Creator—or whoever—if me and Josiah are gonna get married," Erica said. "I'm not bothering The Voice nor the Divine Creator with that. Common sense should tell you to leave that ***thing*** alone!"

Charity and her friends, including Erica, all laughed. "You're right. But he has dimples, and I want our babies to have dimples," Erica pouted. A few moments later, Brittany and her clique went out of their way to walk by Charity's table on their way out of the lunchroom. "I guess that voice in Chasity's head didn't tell her to get up from the dinner table, with her fat butt," Brittany said, as she passed Charity.

The cheerleader's clique laughed and continued to walk out of the lunchroom. "My pastor said that the Divine Creator will talk to anyone who listens," Erica said. "You did your part, Charity. Don't worry about it." "I'm not. I'm going to enjoy all next week being out of school for Spring Break. Like you said, I did my part. I did what this Voice told me to do." The next morning, at approximately nine a.m., Charity awoke to a persistent, repetitive tapping coming from her window.

It scared her so badly that her soul left her body before realizing what the noise was. Groggily, she peeped through the blinds and saw Erica. "Why are you scaring me out of my skin, Erica?!" "I didn't want to wake your parents. I know they sleep in on Saturdays."
"Well, what do you want?"

Erica climbed through the window and sat on Charity's bed. "Brittany was in a bad car wreck early this morning, leaving Lorenzo's party. Her car got wrapped around a tree.

They say she's brain-dead." Charity blinked multiple times, trying to clear the fog out of her brain. She didn't know if she was dreaming, hallucinating, delusional, or so sleepy that she wasn't comprehending, but she couldn't get a grasp on what Erica was telling her. "Wait. Let me go to the bathroom. I gotta pee," Charity said. *Yeah, that was it. Charity couldn't focus with a full bladder. When she would come out of the bathroom, she'd realize that she had heard Erica all wrong. A full bladder was the problem.*

While in the bathroom, she also brushed her teeth. She had to do something with that nervous energy. There was no way Erica said what Charity thought she said. She returned to her room. "Okay. I brushed my teeth, used the bathroom, and washed my hands. What did you say, Erica?"

"Brittany is brain-dead. She was in a car wreck around two this morning when she was leaving Lorenzo's party. Her car got wrapped around a tree. They're saying she was trying to dodge a drunk driver."
"Who are *they*? How do you know this? Who told you? What makes you think they know?" Charity asked, stunned and confused.

"My mom and her mom work nights together over at the hospital. My mama said that all of a sudden, Brittany's mom started screaming and yelling, 'Not my baby! I'm on the way!' My mama is her supervisor and wouldn't let her drive, being so wound up, so my mama drove her to the other hospital, where they took Brittany.

"Mama came home this morning, asking me if I knew a senior named Brittany Perdue, and told me everything that had happened. She said that she even drove Brittany's mom to the scene of the wreck because her mom just wanted to see it, for whatever reason.

Mama said Brittany's brain-dead, and they don't think she's going to make it." Charity began shaking uncontrollably. "I should have talked to her more! I shouldn't have let her leave until she understood how serious The Voice was." "Charity, you did what you were supposed to do. And you have to stop calling it The Voice. It's the Divine Creator. He is talking to you. He is real. And His warnings are real. He chose you because *you listen*. I know you look crazy to people when you tell them that the Divine Creator talks to you. But this is proof. He told you to warn Brittany, and you *did*. She didn't listen, and look what happened. Doesn't the Bible say that warning comes before destruction?" Charity nodded her head. "Okay. You warned her. She didn't listen. Now, she's destroyed."

"Where is she? I gotta go see her." "Okay. I'll walk back home and ask my mom." "Okay. I'll be over there as soon as I get dressed." Charity thought about telling her parents what happened, but she wanted to see for herself first, so she just told them that she and Erica were going to go visit a friend in the hospital, and she'd be back soon. It was a long, quiet ride to the hospital.

Erica drove; Charity didn't have the mental ability to process driving at that time. She wasn't even sure how she ended up on the ICU floor, talking to a nurse. "Well, we usually don't allow more than two visitors at a time, and she already has three. But we are making an exception in her case. Room C5." Charity walked to Brittany's room with Erica holding her hand. As soon as they walked in, all eyes were on them.

"She should've listened to you!" Sheryl, a girl from Brittany's clique who laughed at Charity that day in the lunchroom, roared. "Why didn't she listen? We all should have listened!" Charity stood, planted on the floor, pale as a ghost. Brittany's tubes, machines, wires, and the beeping sounds were all too much for a seventeen-year-old girl who had only seen a blood pressure machine in her life. An older lady who looked like she had spent the last thirteen years of her life crying looked over at Charity and said, "You're her.

The girl they've been telling me about. You knew." No one had to introduce this older lady; she was Brittany's mother. That look of angst and anguish could only belong to a mother. Charity nodded her head "yes" and walked to Brittany. Brittany was… asleep, it appeared.

They were saying she was in a coma, but she looked asleep and bothered. There was a tube going down her throat that was connected to a machine—life support, she was told. "How did you know?" Brittany's mom asked Charity. "I… I just knew. A Voice—the Divine Creator —told me. And He told me to tell her, so I did." "I'm a nurse, Charity," Brittany's mom, Marie, said. "I know this doesn't look good. She is breathing very little on her own.

This machine is the only thing keeping her alive. But I don't want to take her off before giving her a fighting chance. What is this Voice—the Divine Creator telling you now? Do I take her off the machine, or leave her on it?" Charity's stomach flipped inside out and dropped to her toes. Suddenly, there that Voice was again, giving her instructions. How was Charity supposed to tell a mother to let her child die?

"Why me, Oh Divine Creator?" Charity asked the Divine Creator underneath her breath. *"Why not you"?* The Divine Creator asked Charity. Charity sighed and looked around the room. Brittany's mom, her Aunt Margaret, and her friend Sheryl were there, waiting to hear what this Voice had to say. "Just say it, Charity. Be obedient," Erica encouraged her. "This Voice— the Divine Creator—told me to tell you to talk to her right now. Brittany will never be the Brittany that you knew.

 She is fighting right now because she doesn't want to hurt you, but her fighting to stay alive is not helping her at all. The Voice— the Divine Creator —told me to tell you to let her know that it is okay if she is tired and wants to rest with Him. Let her know that you will be okay and that you are not upset with her if she lets go," Charity whispered, shakily. "But why my baby? Why must I bury my child?"

"We all have an end date, Marie. On every tombstone, there's a dash between the birth date and death date. We have to make the dash count. Brittany fulfilled her dash, Marie. Let her know that she can let go," Brittany's Aunt Margaret told Brittany's mom. "I'll hold your hand. Come on. If you love her, you don't want her to suffer."

Brittany's Aunt Margaret and mom walked to Brittany's bedside while holding hands. Her mom grabbed Brittany's hand with her free hand. "My sweet, sweet, adorable, beautiful baby girl. You have always been my miracle, my joy, my blessing. The Divine Creator gave you to me not because you needed me, but because *I* needed *you*. You have been my reason for living for eighteen years. It seems long to you, but seems like a second to me." Marie continued with stories and memories that she and Brittany shared.

Charity learned a lot about Brittany through the stories, like how Brittany was abandoned by her birth mother, and that Marie found her behind a trash can. Charity learned that Brittany fluently spoke three languages: English, Swahili, and French. Brittany won many awards and trophies for playing the piano and tap dancing.

She also found out that Brittany's favorite color was pink, just like hers. In another life, another world, they would have been besties. But this world didn't allow it. Pretty girls like Brittany and chubby girls with acne like Charity didn't belong in the same pot. Marie continued. "What I am saying, Brit Brat, is that you have fulfilled your purpose here. So, if you're tired—" Marie exhaled.

"If this is becoming too much for you if you can't handle this, if you believe there is more peace on the other side, go. Baby, just let go. Be with Jesus.

"I will be okay. I will not be mad at you at all. I will forever be grateful that you stopped in my world eighteen years ago to heal me. And when you are gone, the Divine Creator will heal me.

If you want to, let go, Brit Brat. Let go." Suddenly, the life support machine let out a long piercing beep and read "NO PATIENT EFFORT." Brittany had let go. The gut-wrenching, ear-piercing, skin-crawling screams that Marie let out immediately informed the staff what had happened. They ran in to attempt to resuscitate Brittany, but Marie stopped them. "She's with the Divine Creator now. Let her be," Aunt Margaret told the staff. Marie voiced her agreement to the staff. This was all too much for seventeen-year-old Charity.

She felt that she should leave, but her feet wouldn't let her move. She was staring blankly into oblivion. She couldn't "come to," no matter how hard she tried to snap out of it. "Charity," Sheryl whispered. "Charity, can you hear us?" Erica asked. Aunt Margaret walked to Charity and said, "That Voice will never leave you. Make peace with it now. You have a lifetime ahead of you. You'll have your ups and downs with it. Sometimes people will listen to you, and sometimes they won't. You just make sure *you* listen to it. That's your only job." Charity could only nod.

THE VOICE: MISHAWN CHILDERS

"I will instruct thee and teach thee in the way which thou shalt go: I will guide thee with mine eye." **(Psalm 32:8, KJV)**

Chapter 4
My Brother

Enduring Hard Times and Feeling Trapped

"Chantelle, I'm sick of this. Every time I come around, you always have something to say about who I'm dating. You are paranoid!" "I am *not* paranoid. I am aware, though. You are always messing with these women who have nothing, but require everything.

They bring absolutely nothing to the table except sob stories, negative bank accounts, poor credit, and unkempt children. These kinds of women have agendas, Troy, and I have something to say about these gold-diggers because I am your sister. I care about you! You cannot save them all, and you are going to find out the hard way. I just keep getting this gut feeling, like hearing a Voice in my head that won't shut up, telling me to tell you to leave this woman that you are with."

"You've been telling me to leave Sandy for five years, and nothing has happened yet." "Yet is the key word, your dumb self is gonna hang around, waiting for something to happen, and *when*—not *if*—it does, don't come crying to me. I warned you about her, and you've had enough time to listen.

The Divine Creator has given you time. But instead of using that time to get out and learn how to be by yourself, you have used that time to deepen your situation with Sandy." What Chantelle didn't know was that Troy had broken up with Sandy that morning. Troy invited Chantelle to dinner to tell her about the breakup, but the more they talked, the more he knew she was going to say, "I told you so."

He didn't want to hear it. He wanted to tell his sister how she had been right about everything. But her braggadocious attitude wouldn't let it just be. She would go deep into how he should have listened to her from Day One. How he should have taken her advice. How even though she's younger, she's wiser.

Chantelle wouldn't have noticed how this breakup was tearing him up. She wouldn't have seen how he was trying his hardest to not become undone. The truth was, even though Chantelle was right, and Sandy never loved him, he loved Sandy. He made her his *everything*.

Troy had also given Sandy and her daughter *everything*. He moved them from the projects into his spare condo. He got her off the bus and bought her a brand-new sedan.

He even worked diligently at helping Sandy and her mom restore their relationship, which was shredded into pieces fifteen years before Troy met Sandy. Troy showed Sandy the world. Before him, she had never been outside the city's limits. They went on flights around the world, cruises on the bluest of waters, and taking road trips to the cabins in the mountains.

Then, they had two daughters of their own together. They were a family, just not the "official" kind of family he wanted. He wanted to marry her and live with his wife and children. He wanted to give her his last name, but she said that would interfere with her disability income, so they had remained engaged for the last three-and-a-half years. Things began getting tense between Sandy and Troy a few months prior, ever since Sandy asked Troy to buy her a house.

Troy told her that he wouldn't because she was not his wife. He would not buy a gift so extravagant for her if she wasn't married to him because she could technically decide to leave him at any given moment, and no courts would grant him that house because it was a "gift" from him to her. He might be crazy, but he wasn't stupid. "If I could marry you, I would, Troy! But they would stop my disability if I did!" "So, we are supposed to be boyfriend and girlfriend forever?" "We are engaged.

We're more than boyfriend and girlfriend, Troy, and you know it." "And how long is that supposed to last?" "Til death do us part." "And you're fine with us never being married? Never having the same last name? Fine with us shacking up on the weekends?" "What is a piece of paper anyway, Troy? A piece of paper is not gonna make me love you any more than I already do. It's not gonna make me stay with you forever.

I'm already going to do that, regardless. We don't need a piece of paper to make what we have official. We're already official in our hearts. We have a covenant in our souls. "Some countries don't even have papers to declare them married. Just them being together and loving each other is enough, and we definitely got that. "Plus, we have two girls together. Having two daughters together definitely sealed the deal. We are good. Quit tripping about this marriage paper." The argument would go in circles, repeating itself, accomplishing nothing. Troy would walk away, trying to convince himself that she was right: marriage was just a piece of paper.
But when he'd lie down at night, he knew that it wasn't just a piece of paper. He knew that it was something the Divine Creator required for him to live the right way. He had awakened that morning and just couldn't do it anymore. He was going to give Sandy an ultimatum: marry him or they would break up.

To his surprise, Sandy had her ultimatum that morning: buy her the million-dollar house or she would leave him. In response to her ultimatum, he told her, "Bye." He was not going to bend to her commands any longer. He severed the strings she had that controlled his actions.

He didn't know how he would answer the questions that were sure to come from their girls. They were just two and three years old. He was happy the breakup happened when they were so young and unable to truly process what had happened. But he knew that he'd see Sandy's first daughter, Emily, at some point during the pick-ups and drop-offs of his two daughters, and she'd have questions.

Emily was eight. She had a fairly good amount of understanding. And she had become like his daughter, too. How would he let Emily know that he missed her and that her mom was keeping her away, without making her mom look bad? Emily already had daddy issues. Sandy told her that a specific man was her dad, and then when Sandy got mad at him, Sandy told Emily that he was not her dad.

When Emily told the man about that, he did a DNA test. It was shocking to see the proof that he wasn't Emily's dad. He left Sandy,

THE VOICE: MISHAWN CHILDERS

and Emily hadn't seen him since. Whenever Emily would ask her who her dad was, Sandy would tell her that it wasn't her business.

That night, after the dinner with his sister Chantelle, Troy decided to sleep the day's events off, so he could wake up with a refreshed mind and begin a new journey. **BOOM! BOOM! BOOM!** There was a pounding on Troy's living room door. It didn't sound like someone was using their hand; it sounded like he or she was using a machine or weapon of some sort.

Troy lunged out of bed and headed for his gun—until he saw flashing lights outside his window. He immediately ran to his living room door, panicking, and thinking about his girls. The police must have been at his door about his girls! He looked up—heavenward—and whispered a quick prayer as he opened the door. "Divine Creator, please!" "Troy Taylor?" an officer asked him. "Yes?" "You are under arrest for the aggravated assault with a deadly weapon against Sandy Huffman."

"Aggravated assault with a deadly weapon? What? What are you talking about?" Troy asked incredulously. "Place your hands behind your back, please." "I didn't assault her! I didn't assault anybody!" "Sir, this is the last time that we will ask you to comply, now place your hands behind your back." Troy's world began to spin. He lost his balance, and the officers had to carry him halfway towards the cruiser. Everything was a blur to him.

From the time he found out what he was arrested for to the months he spent rotting inside his cell awaiting trial, everything was one big blur. *I should have listened to my sister. I knew I should have listened to her. All of this is because I wouldn't buy Sandy a house. Why didn't I just listen to my sister?* Sandy came up with an elaborate story of how he attacked her because she wouldn't agree to marry him.

She stated that they got into a heated argument when she refused his proposal. According to her, he pushed her against a wall, then pulled out a knife and held it to her throat in front of the children, threatening to harm her with it. Troy had heard that Sandy told Emily and their two daughters that he was in jail for robbing a bank. They had no idea that Sandy had lied to them. There were no medical records offering proof that Troy had done anything to Sandy. She had no bruises or injuries—nothing! He even passed the lie detector test. It was just his word versus hers. "In the charge of assault with a deadly weapon, we have found Troy Taylor guilty.

Eleven-in-a-half years is your sentence. You will be eligible for parole in eight. You will be transferred to a maximum-security prison to finish your time. The six months that you have served will go towards your time." The gavel banged. Troy temporarily went deaf. His soul cried.

How? How? I'm fifty-two. I will be sixty to sixty-four when I get out. Will life even be worth starting over and living? Will my daughters even know me or love me—or even want to have anything to do with me? Sandy hasn't brought them to visit me, and she never will. What lies is she filling their heads with about me? She won't let my family see my daughters; the little bit of family that I do have left can't even bring my daughters to see me. What will our father-daughter relationships look like?

Will I even have a relationship with them? Day in and day out, it was the same routine: wake up, wash up, work in the prison's kitchen, eat, clean up the prison's kitchen, go to class, play basketball, go to lunch, play cards, go to dinner, take a shower, lights out, lie down, sleep to the best of his ability, and then wake up and do it all over again.

Interwoven between all that was dodging fights, avoiding being stabbed, keeping his head down to not draw any attention to himself, keeping his head up to be aware of his surroundings, standing his ground so that no one would take advantage of him, tiptoeing around the officers, sucking up to the warden, sneaking calls on his hidden cell phone, hiding whatever contraband he was in possession of, crying in the dark, and joking in the light.

In between all of that were the prisoner counts. There was absolutely nowhere that he could go. The walls were cement, the doors were digitally locked, and the fences had barbed wire with electricity flowing through them. The guards counted the inmates a minimum of twelve times a day, and he had to be present every time, even if that meant cutting a bathroom break short so that he could be accounted for.

Walking around the prison with a domestic violence charge was the same as having a target on his back and a laser on his forehead. Abusers of women are not treated well in prison. There was a lot he had to endure. Some things he endured at the hands of the prison's officers, and some things he endured at the hands of the inmates, while the officers either looked the other way—or watched.

Things transpired that he would never tell anyone about. He had to keep a lot to himself because no one cared anyway. To the world, he was a woman beater; he deserved whatever he had coming to him. He had nobody to talk to. His family turned their backs on him because they believed the jury.

His friends had nothing to do with him because they couldn't be associated with a man like him. What if it got out that they were writing, texting, and/or visiting a woman abuser? They didn't want his filth and stains washing onto them. When he checked his social media, he had gone from over seven hundred friends to a mere thirteen. Maybe he should have listened to his sister, but if he had, he wouldn't have had his two beautiful daughters.

Even though Sandy was wrong for him, giving him his daughters is what she did right. So, he couldn't think of Sandy as a mistake. But he wished it didn't turn so ugly. He was grateful that the Divine Creator gave him his two beautiful daughters, but he also wished that he had listened to the Voice that told his sister to tell him to leave Sandy alone.

"Move to Georgia," The Voice told Adelle. "I don't know anyone there. I have a seven-month-old baby. I won't have a babysitter. All of my friends and family are here." *"Your drive, motivation, and talents are too big for this small city in Louisiana. Move to Atlanta, and I will open the doors that you have been praying about. Just go."*

Adelle couldn't. She trusted her fears more than she trusted the Divine Creator. She knew absolutely no one in Atlanta. She had an infant who she only trusted her mom to babysit. She asked her mom to move to Atlanta with her, and her mom said no, so that was that. She wasn't going to put her child in an Atlanta daycare—mainly because she couldn't. Adelle was a nurse who worked twelve-hour shifts, from seven to seven. If she worked from seven a.m. to seven p.m., the daycares closed at six p.m. If she worked from seven p.m. to seven a.m., the daycares would already be closed before she went to work.

Her husband was a nurse who worked twelve hours as well, so he was not a dependable source to care for their daughter while she worked. The few daycares that Adelle and her husband found that were twenty-four hours were run down, and the entire staff was under twenty-five years old. Adelle didn't trust them.

She heard The Voice tell her to move, to pursue her dreams of being an author and a writer who owned a writing business, but she had to tell Him, "No." The Voice told her that if she moved to Atlanta, her writing business would soar, she'd be a household name, and He would blow her mind. But it didn't make sense to her to leave everything and everybody she'd known her whole life. It didn't make sense to her to leave her mom—her babysitter—either.

How would she even begin having a successful business? Where would the building be set up? What would she name the company? What would the colors of the logo be? What would the business's slogan and catchphrase be? Where would she live? How would she advertise? She knew *no one* in Atlanta. And she owned a house in Louisiana. What would she do with that? She didn't know the first thing about selling a home.

She barely knew how to buy a home. Her husband encouraged her to ignore The Voice because none of this made sense. "We are just going to keep working as nurses, saving, praying, and believing that the Divine Creator will enlarge your territory here. We have no one out there. You can write books here the same way you can write books out there. Just promote and advertise more here, and you'll get to where you want to be."

Days turned into months. Months turned into years. Adelle put so much money into promoting and advertising her business: billboards, commercials, magnets for fridges and cars, business cards, and being a vendor at places that held events— only to never see a profit from any of it. The only thing that she received from these investments was people telling her: "I saw your billboard," "I saw your commercial," "I saw a car with your business magnet on it," and "I heard you were downtown at the festival, selling your books and telling people about your publishing company." People were always telling her that they saw her efforts, but no one ever became a client. Her efforts became expensive, excessive, and useless.

Then COVID-19 hit. Adelle heard about the Cares Act that allowed homeowners to put their mortgage loans into default for a little while, meaning they didn't have to pay their mortgage, and it wouldn't affect their credit. Adelle decided that that was the time to listen to The Voice and move to Atlanta as He had instructed her three years earlier. Not having to pay a mortgage allowed her to move to Atlanta and pay for somewhere to live there, all while keeping her home in Louisiana for free—just in case Atlanta didn't work out. Well, it wasn't free.

She still had to pay utilities and HOA fees, but not having to pay a mortgage was a big relief. She decided to rent her house out to help pay for those costs. Before being settled in Atlanta for one full month, Adelle had obtained two clients to ghostwrite for. In Louisiana, it took her two years to get two clients.

After a year, magazines also began noticing her and calling her, hiring her to write for them. Her clientele grew. Her clients began to refer Adelle to their friends and colleagues. It didn't take long for Adelle to know that Atlanta was definitely the place to be for her business to grow and soar. In the beginning, business was up and down.

There were months that she made thousands; there were months that she made hundreds. There were times when she had to go back to working as a nurse for a little while; there were times when writing completely supported her lifestyle. Regardless of the ups and downs, Adelle knew that Louisiana wasn't home anymore. *"Settle here,"* she heard The Voice tell her pertaining to Atlanta. Not settle as in *settling*, getting less than she deserved; but settle, as in stop, rest, and live. Settle, as in stay.

Settle, as in there was nowhere else for Adelle to look or search for because she was right where the Divine Creator designed her to be. After living in Atlanta for three years, the Cares Act was over, meaning that she had to start back paying her mortgage in Louisiana. The renters that she had in her home caused more damage to her home than they paid in rent. After evicting the tenants, Adelle realized that paying for two places to live was hurting her family financially, so she decided to sell her Louisiana home.

The home was an investor's dream, although it was being sold as-is. It wasn't ideal for habitation after the renters moved out, but it definitely could be repaired and flipped. After being on the market for eleven months and not selling, Adelle's money was depleted. She and her husband had to work four jobs between them just to keep afloat. They were still paying rent in Atlanta while continuing to pay the mortgage in Louisiana, plus all the bills that came with both houses: utilities, lawn service, warranties, and etcetera.

They were paying for everything times two. They could not move back into the house in Louisiana because it was uninhabitable after the renters moved out. They couldn't afford to repair it. They especially couldn't move in there having a seven-year-old child.

CPS would be all over that. They couldn't pay the Louisiana mortgage which had a negative impact on their credit. They couldn't pay the Louisiana house's utilities and such because HOA would fine them.

They were stuck. Not only were they paying for two places to live, they still had life's regular bills. Their daughter was in karate, dance, and swim class. They had car loans, car insurance, and health insurance to pay, plus their credit cards. The list went on. Finally, an investment company agreed to buy the house. Now that they had a buyer, Adelle and her husband had to move their remaining belongings out of the house and into a storage unit.

THE VOICE: MISHAWN CHILDERS

They had to pay the movers four hundred dollars that they didn't have, and they had to pay two hundred dollars that they didn't have for storage, but they knew that was better than paying a mortgage for a house that they weren't living in anymore. When the buyers changed their minds and backed out of the contract while they still could, Adelle was crushed and sick.

Not only did this mean that she would have to continue to pay the mortgage and all the house's bills, but she also now had to pay a monthly storage bill as well. Because she moved everything out of the house, she had cut off the Internet. Now, her security cameras no longer work. She had no way to monitor her house now.

"Divine Creator, I did what you told me to do! You told me to leave the comfort of my home in Louisiana and move to Georgia. I did it, and all I have to show for it is embarrassment. I'm back working full-time as a nurse on one job and part-time on my second job. My husband is doing the same. My bank account is the lowest it has been in over a decade. I'm working just to pay bills, and I'm barely paying the bills! What is the purpose? What is the reason? Listening to you has gotten me nowhere!" The Voice answered, *"I told you to move to Atlanta in 2017. You decided you knew more than me and didn't move until 2020. Delayed obedience is still disobedience. You have to suffer the consequences of not doing what I instructed you to do the first time. I will sustain you during this time, but you will suffer. That is the consequence of disobedience."*

The Voice repeated, *"Delayed obedience is still disobedience."* "Then I'm just going to move back to Louisiana. It will be a lot cheaper. If I've managed to pay for two places to live, surely I can manage to pay for only one. I should even have enough money to repair the house and make it habitable again." *"I told you to settle here in Georgia,"* The Voice continued. *"Look at how you are suffering now, all because of your disobedience. Do you really want to be disobedient again and add to the struggle?"* "No," Adelle answered. *"Then learn your lesson from the last time and be obedient this time. Don't forget that delayed obedience is still disobedience."*

"Wherefore, my beloved brethren, let every man be swift to hear, slow to speak, slow to wrath." **(James 1:19, KJV)**

THE VOICE: MISHAWN CHILDERS

Chapter 5: Hidden Enemies

Choosing Healthy Relationships
"It's just hair. It's just hair," Zara whispered to herself, as she shaved her head bald. "I'm still a beautiful woman. Hair does not define me. I am still fearfully and wonderfully made," Zara affirmed herself through tears. With every clump of hair that she witnessed fall to the floor, thirty more tears fell. Just last week, her natural hair was waist-length. Now, on this day, she was literally starting over.

"I knew to leave my so-called best friend alone. Something inside me told me last year to stop going to her, but I didn't listen to that Voice. Why?" Zara asked herself aloud. "Now, look at me. I look like a fool. Many women can pull this look off, but I can't. This isn't for me." A year prior, Zara had shared some intimate details with Michelle about her then-boyfriend. Zara had sworn Michelle to secrecy and trusted that her best friend would never tell a soul, but boy, she was wrong. Michelle shared the information with a couple of their closest friends, and her fiancé found out, which nearly caused them to break up.

They spent months rebuilding trust and are now engaged to be married. *Buzz.* Her clippers sent the last clump of hair to the floor. *"She's jealous of you,"* The Voice whispered to her in the middle of the night last year. *"Your best friend is so jealous of you. You have a wonderful fiancé, you excel at everything, and your family is well-known and loved. She not only wants what you have, she wants to be you. She is jealous of you, can you not see that? She won't kill you, but one day, she'll make you wish you were dead."*

That day was today. She kept replaying her last interaction with her friend in her head. She wanted a hairstyle to showcase her long tresses. Zara and her fiancé were planning a European vacation, and she was also excited about the opportunity of being a hair model.

She had applied to become one, months prior. Therefore, she was so excited that she couldn't stop sharing the vacation details with

Michelle, along with the possibility of being a hair model for a brand she had used for years. Everything was working out in her favor and she decided that a day of pampering herself at her friend's salon before the vacation would be perfect.

Little did she know how wrong she would be! The hairstylist's friend, Michelle, took one look at Zara's hair and said, "Your hair needs a protein treatment. Your hair is shedding. A protein treatment will stop it from shedding any further." Zara hadn't noticed her hair shedding, but she trusted the professional. She agreed to receive the protein treatment.

Within ten minutes of the protein treatment being on her hair, her scalp began burning. It felt like literal flames were doing what they were created to do. "Michelle! This burns!" "That just means that it's working." "I don't think so. I've had protein treatments before, and none of them felt like this." Zara panicked. "That's because your hair was never this damaged. Just let it do what it's supposed to do."

Zara internally cried from the pain and trusted the process and the professional. When Michelle rinsed the protein treatment out of Zara's hair, the water felt like gasoline on Zara's scalp. The burning intensified, and Zara couldn't contain her screams. At the end of the appointment, Zara's hair was dry and stiff. Her hair looked like a cross between a bird's nest and hay. Her hair could not move; styling it was not even an option. "My hair is like straw!" Zara yelled as she pushed her hair back, only for it to shoot back up. "What did you do, Michelle? Fix it!" Nonchalantly, Michelle asked her, "What did you eat today?" "Nothing! I had coffee and headache medicine. What does that have to do with anything?" "That's the problem. You had caffeine and no nourishment. No wonder this happened to your hair." "That is bull, and you know it!"

Zara was willing to blame it on the product being defective. But when Michelle displayed a nonchalant, lackadaisical, carefree attitude, Zara was convinced that it was the "friend" who was defective, not the product. "That will be eighty dollars," Michelle told her. "Eighty dollars for you messing my hair up? You can't even style it because of whatever you did! I'm not paying you anything!

As a matter of fact, you owe me!" "No, Zara. I did the work. You wanted the protein treatment, and you got it," Michelle rebutted. "You're the one who suggested it!" "I didn't put a gun to your head. You could have told me, 'No.'"

Never in Zara's life had she ever wanted to put her hands on someone. She was never a fighter or a violent person. Fighting, arguing, going back and forth with a person, and having screaming matches—all of that seemed useless and stupid... until today.
She now understood the overwhelming, uncontrollable desire to pummel someone's face in. It wasn't about hair anymore but about love, friendship, accountability, respect, honor, and humility—all the things Michelle did not have. She even lacked being apologetic and sympathetic. Michelle didn't acknowledge her fault in any of this, in any capacity. She had to answer for this. Zara was a high-esteemed woman, and her name carried weight.

Her fighting in a beauty shop—or anywhere else—would have been breaking news. Everything that she and her family had spent years working towards and building would have been dismantled in a matter of seconds if Zara hadn't control her temper. But paying Michelle eighty dollars? She could not. And she did not. Zara stomped out of the salon so fiercely that Michelle was too afraid to demand Zara to pay.

Zara spent two weeks Googling solutions and trying different things to bring her hair back. Nothing restored it. Nothing! Her hair remained a ball of hay and tumbleweed. There was only one solution left that she hadn't tried: cut it off and start over. *I might as well accept it. It is what it is. It's not going to come back overnight. Just deal with it, Zara*, she told herself after cutting all of her hair off. She laid on the couch to soak in her new life.

She did her best to look at the bright side of things. *At least I get a brand new start in life. That hair was attached to my old job, all the stresses of the past, and all the pain I have been through, including my mom's death. I cut off all of my life's pain with the hair*. She was doing her best to encourage herself when the phone rang. "Hello?" Zara answered. "May I speak with Ms. Zara Stewart?" "This is she."

THE VOICE: MISHAWN CHILDERS

"Hi! This is Lori Eagle from Go Me Natural Hair Casting. We received your application and pictures of your beautiful waist-long hair. You have been using our hair products for ten years, according to your application, correct?" "Yes," Zara whispered. "You are the perfect candidate to be our model-promoter. I can see you now, sashaying down the runway and slinging that beautiful hair from side to side." Lori took a few seconds to smile and bask in the vision. "I see that you are living in Arkansas right now.

We will fly you out to London, England; all expenses paid, and have you travel with us for about three months during the summer time. "The time frame really depends on the success of this launch. We are a big deal in America, and now, we're trying to be a big deal in the UK. So, I am saying you'll be in London for three months because that is what is projected, but that can change. It may be three months or longer but only if that works for you. We don't know, but we will definitely work with you.

"But the contract that I will email you binds you for three months. Once again, as I mentioned before, we will pay for everything! We'll pay for everything from your plane ticket, housing, and meals to your transportation, for the entire time you're there. "In addition to that, we will give you three hundred dollars a day that will be distributed to you every other Thursday. You will receive that on your Visa debit that we will give you. "All of this information and other information will be in the email that I am sending if you choose to accept this promotion.

"But I will tell you that a major downside to this—other than living in a foreign country away from everyone you know and love—is that you are almost guaranteed to work every Saturday. Because the runway shows and events are almost always on Saturdays, your Saturdays belong to us, from before the sun is up until after the sun is down. After the shows and events, we have meetings, appearances, etcetera.

"We don't do too much on Sundays, so if you're a churchgoer, that will work for you. Your Mondays will be dedicated to Corporate…" Zara faded out. She had stopped hearing Lori minutes ago. Zara was unmarried with no children. Her dream was to live it up in London, without a care in the world. Every night in her dreams, she was a hair model for this Go Me brand that she had been buying and using for the last ten years.

She was living proof that this brand worked. The only thing it couldn't do was reverse the damage of whatever Michelle had done, but the brand was not to blame for that. Zara had applied to be a hair model for them months ago. She had forgotten about it, honestly. And of all days for them to call… Zara interrupted Lori, "Ma'am, my hairstylist put some kind of chemicals in my hair that made it hard and full of knots. Today, I had to cut my hair off at the scalp and start over."

"Oh, no! What…" Lori's voice drifted off. "Is there a way I can still be a hair model for Go Me and visually document the growth and health progress and process? I mean, I am basically bald, so that will display the product's worth—showing how quickly the products are making my hair grow." Zara bit the inside of her mouth as she awaited Lori's answer. She didn't have to wait long. Lori already knew her answer. "No, Ma'am. Like I said, this could be a short launch—three months.

As great as our product is, your hair will not be waist-length in three months. It won't even be shoulder-length. I'm sorry. You are not the ideal candidate, and we will not be proceeding with you. "But best of luck on your hair journey. I hope you continue to use our product and tell all your friends, families, and associates the good things about us. Have a wonderful day. Bye-bye."

Lori hung up the phone before allowing Zara to say anything else. All within a matter of minutes, Zara lost her hair *and* a once-in-a-lifetime opportunity. She now understood when the voice told her, *"Allowing someone full of hate, envy, and jealousy close access to you is the same as putting your life in her hands. You won't die, but you will wish that you were dead."* If only she'd listened to The Voice.

"He therefore that despiseth, despiseth not man, but the Divine Creator, who hath also given unto us his Holy Spirit." (1 Thessalonians 4:8, KJV)

THE VOICE: MISHAWN CHILDERS

Chapter 6
The Whisper

When God Speaks, We Should Listen

"I'm sorry, Charlotte," Penny apologized to her sister over the phone. "Paul was supposed to be here two hours ago to pick up our daughters. I have tried calling and calling, but of course, he's not answering. I'm just going to cancel our outing tonight. Even if he showed up right now, that doesn't leave enough time for me to get dressed and ready."

Charlotte huffed. "Penny, we planned this almost a year ago." "I know. But what do you want me to do? This is Paul's weekend to get the kids, and he hasn't shown up. My girls are six and eight. I can't leave them here by themselves." *"Go to his house and check on him,"* Penny heard a Voice tell her. Penny argued with The Voice in her head. *Check on him for what? He knows that it's his weekend to keep his kids. He's a grown man, and I'm not chasing him. He either does what he's supposed to do, or he doesn't. I'm not arguing with him anymore.*

"Ask Mom to keep them," Charlotte suggested to Penny. Penny rolled her eyes. "I can hear you rolling your eyes through the phone, Penny. Just ask her." "You ask her. You're her favorite." "I sure will," Charlotte said. "Even if she agrees to, like I said, there is no time left for me to get ready. I still have to go to the nail shop." "Girl, this is a sold-out concert. I promise you, no one will notice your nails. No one cares about your toes. No one will even notice you. No one is there to see you." Penny exhaled. "Points were made." Penny and Charlotte laughed. "Okay. I am about to bathe and will be putting your nieces in the car in about an hour. I know Mom isn't going to tell you no, so I already have it in my mind that the girls are going over to her house."

"You know she won't tell me no. I'm the only child she loves," Charlotte joked. "I'll meet you at Mom's house, and we'll leave together from there. See you in a little bit." *"Check on Paul,"* The Voice told Penny again. Penny chuckled at the absurdity of checking on Paul. He was her ex-husband, and she capitalized on that. "Ex" meant that he was no longer her concern, and she no longer had to "check on him." The courts had granted her freedom from him being a priority in her life. If it had nothing to do with their kids, she had nothing to do with him. Her mom was going to watch her girls; she especially didn't need to go *check on him*. Penny bathed and put on her makeup. She hated having her mom do anything for her, but she really needed this sister-sister time. And if she missed this concert with her sister, she would never hear the end of it. She packed her daughters in her car and headed towards her mother's house. She didn't get confirmation from Charlotte that her mom would watch her daughters, but Penny didn't care; her daughters were going to her mom's.

She pulled into her mom's driveway. Charlotte ran out, hugging her and the girls. Her mom stood in the doorway with her arms wide open for her granddaughters. "Let's go. You don't even need to walk in the house," Charlotte told Penny. As they were driving to the concert that they had waited nine months to attend and paid three hundred dollars apiece for, Penny heard The Voice again. *"Check on Paul at his house."* Penny angrily exhaled. "Paul was a horrible husband, but he has always been a great father. I still have not heard from him. This is not like him," Penny told Charlotte. "I was thinking about that. You are right. He always *has* been a great father.

He wouldn't just not show up for his girls. Something might be wrong." Penny called Paul's neighbor Greg. "Hey, Greg. This is Penelope, Paul's ex-wife. I haven't heard from him today. He was supposed to pick the girls up. It's not like him to not show up. Are you able to check on him right now?"

"Hey, Penny. Sure, I'll go check on him. I'll call you right back." "Okay. Thanks." Penny kept driving towards the concert and chewed the inside of her jaws until Greg called her back. "Penny," Greg said over the car's Bluetooth, once Penny answered his call. Penny could hear the panic in his voice. "What?" "I just called nine-one-one. He's on the living room floor, not able to move or talk. He didn't even seem to understand what I was saying.

He's breathing and awake, but I think he had a stroke." Penny slammed on the brakes. She couldn't think or focus. "I'll drive,"

THE VOICE: MISHAWN CHILDERS

Charlotte told Penny. Then she added, "Greg, tell the paramedics that we will meet them at the county hospital." The entire drive there, Penny cried and screamed. *"I should've listened! I should've listened! Something inside me kept telling me to check on him. I should've listened!"*

"Penny, don't do this to yourself. There was no way for you to know that he was in this condition. How many times have you told him to get those headaches checked out? How many times have you told him that he needs to be on blood pressure medicine? You did your part." Penny shook her head. "No, I didn't. I should've listened to The Voice when it told me to go to his house and check on him." Penny and Charlotte met the paramedics and Paul at the county hospital.

Paul was rushed into surgery. After hours of pacing and waiting, the surgeon had an update for Penny. "Paul had a hemorrhagic stroke. That is usually caused by high blood pressure. I didn't see a diagnosis of hypertension anywhere in his charts. Do you know if he had high blood pressure?" "Every time I checked his blood pressure, it was high. He complained about headaches all the time. I told him a million times to go to the doctor," Penny said.

Tears began flooding her face again. "He should have listened to you. You know, we call hypertension 'the silent killer.' A lot of people who have high blood pressure don't have symptoms at all—or the symptoms are so subtle, like a headache, that it doesn't get their attention. Most adults will not stop their busy lives for a headache. We think that we can shoo away a headache. We think that if the high blood pressure is only causing a headache, it's not bad. But we don't see the internal damage that high blood pressure is doing.

A headache is the thunder that lets us know a hurricane is on its way. "But the good news is we stopped the bleeding in his brain. He is out of surgery, but he is paralyzed on his right side, and there is a strong possibility that he will never regain function on his right side." Penny's knees failed her, and she crumbled to the ground.

"His speech, more than likely, will be slurred. He will have trouble forming words. He will have clear thoughts, but he won't be able to always find the words to verbalize them. "There will also be times that he has the words, but they won't be clear. For example, I asked him his name, and if I didn't know that his name was Paul, I wouldn't have understood what he said. "He has months, maybe years, of physical, occupational, and speech therapy ahead of him.

He may even choke on water and other thin liquids and will need to have his liquids thickened to be able to swallow them. "He has a long road to recovery. He will have to learn to walk with a cane and walker. He will need to use a wheelchair. Small things like shaving will be a challenge for him. "Of course, I am making broad, blanket statements. At the end of the day, we will know for sure, when he begins getting back to life. And as far as recovery… only time will tell.

"He is awake now. I have told him what I have told you. You are more than welcome to go be with him." Penny entered Paul's room. The room felt so cold. Not the temperature, but the climate, the aura, the atmosphere. And it was so heavy. The weight was unbearable. Just yesterday, Paul was a thirty-six-year-young man, mowing his yard to make sure there were no snakes that would bite his daughters when they came over on the weekend. And the next day, he became a thirty-six-year-old man who was incoherently sputtering out his name. How?

When Penny walked into Paul's hospital room, she saw tears lined his cheeks. They wouldn't stop flowing, and it didn't appear that he was trying to make them stop. *If he sees you crying, he'll lose whatever little bit of hope he has left,* Penny thought to herself.

"Paul. Hi." He looked through her, not at her. He was just… there… trying to digest this. "If you didn't want to get the girls this weekend, that's all you had to say. This was a bit excessive." Paul chuckled and nodded his head. Dark humor was always the way he coped. Penny hated dark humor.

She couldn't understand how anyone could laugh at such things. But she stooped to dark humor's level this day. She needed her children's father to laugh and be his normal, goofy self again. "I— it—I— shoot!" Paul hit his lap with his left hand out of frustration. "What,

THE VOICE: MISHAWN CHILDERS

Paul? I'm listening. Tell me." "I—it—see—ugh!" "You can tell me anything. Why are you not talking? Just say—" Penny stopped talking.

She remembered that the doctor said that he would have clear thoughts but wouldn't be able to form the words. That was happening. This was real. The frustration that rushed through Paul's veins was palpable.

He felt trapped inside of his own body. The thoughts were clearly there, but the words just wouldn't form. He squeezed his eyes to make the words form, but they never did. He focused hard on forming the words, but the words never came.

He prayed, cried, and cursed in his head to push the words out, but the words still never came. He felt as though he were buried alive, suffocating in his thoughts, drowning in his feelings, being tormented from reliving situations over and over in his mind, and being tortured by the voices in his head.

The Voice had told him over and over to go to the doctor to check on his headache, but he didn't listen. The Voice had urged him in the middle of some nights to go to the ER when the headaches began altering his vision. The Voice had told him multiple times throughout the years to take better care of his health: walk thirty minutes every day, reduce stress, reduce his fat intake, and increase fruits and vegetables.

The Voice had told him many times throughout the years to take blood pressure medicine until his diet and lifestyle made him healthy enough to not require medication. Yet, he ignored it.

The Voice had spoken to him every morning for the past week, too, prior to his stroke. It clearly said, *"Call in sick to work, and go to the hospital to have your headache evaluated."* Yet he continued to ignore The Voice. Paul thought, *If I would have just gone to the doctor if I just would have taken whatever medicine they prescribed me, and if I would have just listened to The Voice, I wouldn't be a thirty-six-year-old invalid who needs his daughters to feed him and his ex-wife to shave him.* But it was just a headache.

THE VOICE: MISHAWN CHILDERS

Who stops their life for a headache? Not many! They might just take some acetaminophen and lie down. If that didn't work, they might add some ibuprofen, and sit in a dark, quiet room or sleep it off. Time heals everything, right? It will eventually go away, right? It was just a headache. Over time, after Paul left the hospital, physical therapy revived him, but it didn't restore him. Occupational therapy helped him, but it didn't heal him. Speech therapy made him better, but he was still bitter.

He was confined to a wheelchair for anything that required true distance. He had to learn to write with his left hand, yet his writing never became legible. Although he had a brilliant mind, his carpentry job required the use of his hands, not his thoughts. Even if they utilized his thoughts, he couldn't always fully verbally express them anyway. He missed eating his favorite foods.

Paralysis from the stroke left him not being able to swallow a lot of foods and beverages. The most demeaning thing of them all was that he never regained control over his bodily functions; he never knew when he had to go to the bathroom or when he had already "gone to the bathroom." Years later, when his daughters got married, they had to push him down the aisle, instead of walking down the aisle beside them. They rolled him around in his wheelchair on the dance floor for their first dance.

He couldn't effectively give a speech at their weddings the way their mom could. When his dad died, he couldn't give the eulogy the way his broken heart desired to, as a last "thank you" to such an awesome man. At fifty-eight, twenty-two years later, he still couldn't swallow well, and he choked while drinking milk.

He developed pneumonia from that incident, and his body never recovered. As he lay on his deathbed, he thought about how if he had checked on his headaches, he would have been given blood pressure medication. If he had taken the medication, he wouldn't have had the stroke. If he wouldn't have had the stroke, he wouldn't have had difficulty swallowing or choking on the milk that ultimately gave him pneumonia. If he didn't have pneumonia, he wouldn't be dying in his fifties. Paul's final thought before he died was: *I should have listened to The Voice.*

"Beloved, believe not every spirit, but try the spirits whether they are of the Divine Creator: because many false prophets are gone out into the world." **(1 John 4:1, KJV)**

THE VOICE: MISHAWN CHILDERS

Chapter 7: Moving On

Listening to God for Direction and Guidance

"Move to Georgia," The Voice told Adelle. "I don't know anyone there. I have a seven-month-old baby. I won't have a babysitter. All of my friends and family are here." *"Your drive, motivation, and talents are too big for this small city in Louisiana. Move to Atlanta, and I will open the doors that you have been praying about. Just go."*

Adelle couldn't. She trusted her fears more than she trusted the Divine Creator. She knew absolutely no one in Atlanta. She had an infant who she only trusted her mom to babysit. She asked her mom to move to Atlanta with her, and her mom said no, so that was that. She wasn't going to put her child in an Atlanta daycare—mainly because she couldn't. Adelle was a nurse who worked twelve-hour shifts, from seven to seven. If she worked from seven a.m. to seven p.m., the daycares closed at six p.m. If she worked from seven p.m. to seven a.m., the daycares would already be closed before she went to work.

Her husband was a nurse who worked twelve hours as well, so he was not a dependable source to care for their daughter while she worked. The few daycares that Adelle and her husband found that were twenty-four hours were run down, and the entire staff was under twenty-five years old. Adelle didn't trust them. She heard The Voice tell her to move, to pursue her dreams of being an author and a writer who owned a writing business, but she had to tell Him, "No."

The Voice told her that if she moved to Atlanta, her writing business would soar, she'd be a household name, and He would blow her mind. But it didn't make sense to her to leave everything and everybody she'd known her whole life. It didn't make sense to her to leave her mom—her babysitter—either.

How would she even begin having a successful business? Where would the building be set up? What would she name the company?

THE VOICE: MISHAWN CHILDERS

What would the colors of the logo be? What would the business's slogan and catchphrase be? Where would she live? How would she advertise? She knew *no one* in Atlanta. And she owned a house in Louisiana. What would she do with that? She didn't know the first thing about selling a home. She barely knew how to buy a home. Her husband encouraged her to ignore The Voice because none of this made sense.

"We are just going to keep working as nurses, saving, praying, and believing that the Divine Creator will enlarge your territory here. We have no one out there. You can write books here the same way you can write books out there. Just promote and advertise more here, and you'll get to where you want to be."

Days turned into months. Months turned into years. Adelle put so much money into promoting and advertising her business: billboards, commercials, magnets for fridges and cars, business cards, and being a vendor at places that held events— only to never see a profit from any of it. The only thing that she received from these investments was people telling her: "I saw your billboard," "I saw your commercial," "I saw a car with your business magnet on it," and "I heard you were downtown at the festival, selling your books and telling people about your publishing company." People were always telling her that they saw her efforts, but no one ever became a client. Her efforts became expensive, excessive, and useless.

Then COVID-19 hit. Adelle heard about the Cares Act that allowed homeowners to put their mortgage loans into default for a little while, meaning they didn't have to pay their mortgage, and it wouldn't affect their credit. Adelle decided that that was the time to listen to The Voice and move to Atlanta as He had instructed her three years earlier.

Not having to pay a mortgage allowed her to move to Atlanta and pay for somewhere to live there, all while keeping her home in Louisiana for free—just in case Atlanta didn't work out. Well, it wasn't free. She still had to pay utilities and HOA fees, but not having to pay a mortgage was a big relief.

THE VOICE: MISHAWN CHILDERS

She decided to rent her house out to help pay for those costs. Before being settled in Atlanta for one full month, Adelle had obtained two clients to ghostwrite for. In Louisiana, it took her two years to get two clients.

After a year, magazines also began noticing her and calling her, hiring her to write for them. Her clientele grew. Her clients began to refer Adelle to their friends and colleagues. It didn't take long for Adelle to know that Atlanta was definitely the place to be for her business to grow and soar. In the beginning, business was up and down. There were months that she made thousands; there were months that she made hundreds.

There were times when she had to go back to working as a nurse for a little while; there were times when writing completely supported her lifestyle. Regardless of the ups and downs, Adelle knew that Louisiana wasn't home anymore. *"Settle here,"* she heard The Voice tell her pertaining to Atlanta. Not settle as in *settling*, getting less than she deserved; but settle, as in stop, rest, and live. Settle, as in stay. Settle, as in there was nowhere else for Adelle to look or search for because she was right where the Divine Creator designed her to be. After living in Atlanta for three years, the Cares Act was over, meaning that she had to start back paying her mortgage in Louisiana. The renters that she had in her home caused more damage to her home than they paid in rent. After evicting the tenants, Adelle realized that paying for two places to live was hurting her family financially, so she decided to sell her Louisiana home.

The home was an investor's dream, although it was being sold as-is. It wasn't ideal for habitation after the renters moved out, but it definitely could be repaired and flipped. After being on the market for eleven months and not selling, Adelle's money was depleted.

She and her husband had to work four jobs between them just to keep afloat. They were still paying rent in Atlanta while continuing to pay the mortgage in Louisiana, plus all the bills that came with both houses: utilities, lawn service, warranties, and etcetera.

They were paying for everything times two. They could not move back into the house in Louisiana because it was uninhabitable after the renters moved out. They couldn't afford to repair it. They especially couldn't move in there having a seven-year-old child. CPS would be all over that. They couldn't pay the Louisiana mortgage which had a negative impact on their credit. They couldn't pay the Louisiana house's utilities and such because HOA would fine them.

They were stuck. Not only were they paying for two places to live, they still had life's regular bills. Their daughter was in karate, dance, and swim class. They had car loans, car insurance, and health insurance to pay, plus their credit cards. The list went on. Finally, an investment company agreed to buy the house. Now that they had a buyer, Adelle and her husband had to move their remaining belongings out of the house and into a storage unit.

They had to pay the movers four hundred dollars that they didn't have, and they had to pay two hundred dollars that they didn't have for storage, but they knew that was better than paying a mortgage for a house that they weren't living in anymore. When the buyers changed their minds and backed out of the contract while they still could, Adelle was crushed and sick.

Not only did this mean that she would have to continue to pay the mortgage and all the house's bills, but she also now had to pay a monthly storage bill as well. Because she moved everything out of the house, she had cut off the Internet. Now, her security cameras no longer work. She had no way to monitor her house now.

"Divine Creator, I did what you told me to do! You told me to leave the comfort of my home in Louisiana and move to Georgia. I did it, and all I have to show for it is embarrassment. I'm back working full-time as a nurse on one job and part-time on my second job. My husband is doing the same. My bank account is the lowest it has been in over a decade. I'm working just to pay bills, and I'm barely paying the bills! What is the purpose? What is the reason? Listening to you has gotten me nowhere!"

THE VOICE: MISHAWN CHILDERS

The Voice answered, *"I told you to move to Atlanta in 2017. You decided you knew more than me and didn't move until 2020. Delayed obedience is still disobedience. You have to suffer the consequences of not doing what I instructed you to do the first time. I will sustain you during this time, but you will suffer. That is the consequence of disobedience."*

The Voice repeated, *"Delayed obedience is still disobedience."* "Then I'm just going to move back to Louisiana. It will be a lot cheaper. If I've managed to pay for two places to live, surely I can manage to pay for only one. I should even have enough money to repair the house and make it habitable again." *"I told you to settle here in Georgia,"* The Voice continued. *"Look at how you are suffering now, all because of your disobedience. Do you really want to be disobedient again and add to the struggle?"* "No," Adelle answered. *"Then learn your lesson from the last time and be obedient this time. Don't forget that delayed obedience is still disobedience."*

*"But he said, yea rather, blessed are they that hear the word of the Divine Creator, and keep it." * **(Luke 11:28, KJV)**

THE VOICE: MISHAWN CHILDERS

Chapter 8: The Present

Walking in Prosperity Through God's Voice

"Mia, have you lost your mind? You haven't been anywhere in your life. You've never even been to the Walmart up the street because you are too afraid to cross a street. But you are going to move from our midsized town of Lubbock, Texas, to the huge town of Dallas, Texas? It may be the same state, but that's a whole different country. You will go there and drown!"

Mia's aunt continued, unrelentingly, "Traffic is atrocious. The people don't have Southern hospitality because most of them aren't even from the south. The food is trash because there are so many people there that the restaurants don't take their time cooking the food because they have to rush and get it out so fast. "And you have a daughter!

Not only will the school system fail her out there because she will just become another number in the crowd, but you will never get a man out there, being a single mother. Here, men understand situations like yours and are accepting. In Dallas, there are too many women to pick from for them to settle for you—a single mother whose baby daddy is alive but doing nothing for his child.

"You are only twenty-five years old. You are just now able to legally rent a car on your own without a penalty from the insurance company. You've never lived on your own. Even those few semesters in college when you moved away, you had a roommate. What would possess you to move, girl?" "This Voice just won't leave me alone, Auntie. It wakes me up at night.

When I'm eating, I hear it. When I'm cleaning, I hear it. When I'm working, I hear it. The Voice won't let up. I know it is the Divine Creator. It definitely isn't me or my conscience! "You are right. I am terrified to leave. I haven't been anywhere in my life.

THE VOICE: MISHAWN CHILDERS

If I could have it my way, I would stay here with you and Uncle James for the rest of my life. But I know that the Divine Creator has more in store for me. "Maybe I keep going in circles because I need to change my environment. It is crazy for me to expect something new when I keep doing the same thing.

Maybe, just maybe, Dallas is the game-changer. Maybe Dallas is the answer. "All I do is work, pay bills, go to work to be able to pay more bills and pay bills so that I can have what I need to go to work. This cycle has me tired. "I have a seven-year-old daughter who only sees me on Sunday mornings, right before I go to work. This cannot be life.

I understand rough seasons and dry patches. This is not a season or a patch, though. This has become the definition of me. "I hear you, Aunt Patty. I really do. But I'm leaving. That Voice belongs to the Divine Creator. I know it. And I'm listening this time."

Outside of the one-hundred-dollar gas card that her job had given her as a going-away gift, Mia had twenty-five dollars and thirteen cents to her name. And that was only because she had forgotten to pay her cell phone bill two days ago. If she had paid it, her account would have been in the negative. She knew that the cell phone company would give her a ten-day grace period. What would she do in seven days? She had no idea. She'd cross that bridge when she got there.

She packed her seven-year-old daughter, Lydia, in the car along with three suitcases, two blankets, and Lydia's "Lovie." Lydia could go nowhere without her Lovie. Mia made sure that Lydia's Lovie was the first thing that she packed. She would turn around on two wheels and go back to get it if she left it.

This move was going to be stressful on Lydia; she was going to need her Lovie to get her through it all. Mia was beginning to wish that she had a Lovie herself; a stuffed animal, a pink throw, a satin pillowcase, a doll—something! But she had The Voice guiding her, and she had learned that that was enough. They got to Dallas and settled into the studio apartment that was waiting for her. Her job had given her a surprise bonus, and she used that money to pay the down payment on the apartment, turn on the utilities, and pay the first month's rent. How

THE VOICE: MISHAWN CHILDERS

she was going to pay the second month's rent was unknown. She'd cross that bridge when she got there.

She had a job waiting for her that paid eight more dollars an hour than her last job. She knew that it'd be three weeks before she received a paycheck and that it wouldn't be a full check. The bills were steadily coming, her mind was continuing to whirl, and yet The Voice kept telling her to keep going. "Mommy, I don't know if you need this, but my school gave this to me today.

My teacher said they give it to all new students who move in from out of town." Mia looked at the paper, front and back. It was a paper full of coupons, discounts, and freebies, ranging from free burgers and fries at McDonald's to a one-month free Internet service for new and existing customers to a ten-percent discount off of a car if she shopped at a certain dealership. She could not believe that there were also coupons for utilities.

She had never seen anything like that before in her life. She had no problem being on the phone all day the next day to receive her free month of the Internet, thirty dollars off of her light bill, fifty dollars off her cell phone bill, and more. Everything was falling in her lap and falling into place.

Her fourth day in Dallas was her first day at her new job. She was hired to be a receptionist at a law firm. It wasn't her dream job, but a job was a job. It was also a job that allowed her to put her daughter on the school bus in the morning and be there when she got off it in the afternoon. It paid more than anything she'd ever received in her life. She was going to make it work. "Hi, Ms. Ramos. I am Attorney Johnson. Thank you for coming to orientation. Can we talk in my office?" Mia looked around, confused.

She saw the look on Attorney Johnson's face. He'd changed his mind about hiring her; she just knew it. Now she would have to go back to Lubbock with her tail between her legs and tell Aunt Patty that she was right; her moving to Dallas was the stupidest thing she could have ever done. As Mia followed Attorney Johnson to his office, she had to remind herself to pick her head up. She felt defeated, but she didn't have to look like it.

"Once again, thank you for coming. I'm going to get straight to it. My nephew has three children. He lost his job yesterday. He is on parole, and he has to keep a job. I gave him your receptionist position." *Thud.* Mia's heart dropped into her stomach. "As a result of that, my legal assistant quit. She said that she wasn't comfortable working so closely with a felon. My nephew went to prison for armed robbery and aggravated assault."

Mia nodded her head, swallowing her vomit. She honestly didn't care about the nephew, the legal assistant, and the computers, the birds outside, the desks, the chairs, or the cars on the highway. She didn't care about anything, except her daughter, who deserved the world. Now, Mia might not even be able to give her a bedroom! "I wanted you to know what happened to your position. I also wanted you to know that a felon will be in the building if you accept my offer to be a legal assistant for my team.

"Mia had to run the conversation back through her head. She was so busy blinking away tears that she almost didn't catch on to the fact that she was just offered a higher position.

"Legal assistant? I would love it, but I am not certified enough for that position. I don't even have a degree." "That is okay. I do on-the-job training. There is no degree needed to be a legal assistant. You are probably thinking about a paralegal. But my paralegal will be the one training you. The receptionist job paid eighteen dollars an hour. Being a legal assistant pays twenty-two dollars an hour. Do you accept?"

Mia's head was reeling. She made ten dollars an hour mopping the floors at a flea market in Lubbock, Texas. Twenty-two dollars an hour sounded like millionaire status. She grinned. "I accept." "Another thing. Can you still start today? I need a legal assistant badly." "I sure can. But just like when I was going to have the receptionist's position, I have to be off by three so that I can get my daughter off the bus at three forty-five." "I understand that. I have five children myself. I know you just moved here, so I'm not sure if you're aware, and I'm not trying to overstep any boundaries.

I mean this in the most respectful way. It's just that at one point, I moved somewhere new and had to establish residency and all that. In the meantime, I knew nothing, and I was as broke as stepped-on crackers." Mia didn't mean to laugh, but she was in that situation at the present time, and she had to laugh to keep from crying. "I'm serious." Attorney Johnson laughed back. "I was so down, I had to look up to see my shoes." Mia exhaled in agreement. "I was a single dad at the time.

My girlfriend had gotten arrested and went to federal prison for nine years. Anyway, another story, another time. "My point is, I needed help. I know that summer is coming. In the event that you don't have a summer camp or anything for your daughter, every summer, my church has free camp from six in the morning until seven at night. They go on field trips to parks, explore the city, and learn Bible stories. If they raise enough money through fundraising, they even go to Six Flags, Disney World, and places like that.

A few years ago, the church was able to take the kids and their parents to the Jordan River. A few parents and children even got baptized in the Jordan River. They had some huge donors that year."
"As in *the* Jordan River?" "*The* Jordan River. It was a sight, I tell ya! My church lets only the first one hundred and five kids in. It's first come, first serve. The waiting list opens up this Sunday after church.

We are a small church, but it's like the word gets out when sign-up time comes, and everyone from miles around comes to church that day. So, I highly suggest you come on Sunday, and sit on the back pew so that you can be the first out the door into the lobby to sign up." "Do I have to be a member?" "No. It's open to the community. And believe me, the community will be there this Sunday, signing their kids up."

"Oh, wow! Thank you so much! I seriously had no idea what I would do about this summer. I guess I was just going to send her back home to be with my aunt and uncle. But I'd love for her to have a summer with other children. She's an only child, and she has started to ask for a sibling. I can't give her a sibling, but I can give her a community of kids."

Mia, in fact, hadn't even thought that far ahead about the summer. It was January, and summer break was the furthest thing from her mind. Whenever that time came, she would figure it out, like she always did. But by the grace of the Divine Creator, she wouldn't have to "figure it out" this time. "Like I said, I didn't mean to offend you in any way. I just know what it's like being the new kid on the block with a child. It's rough." "No offense taken, at all! Thank you so much!" "You're welcome. And in the summer, you will be able to come in to work earlier and stay later if you want.

With you having to come in later and leave earlier because of getting your daughter on and off the bus, you won't be getting forty hours a week. But in the summer, you'll have a babysitter all that time because of summer camp, and you'll be able to work more. Only if you want to, though. I don't mind having to pay you for forty hours." Attorney Johnson smiled. "I'm getting my forty hours, come summertime!" Mia smiled back.

Her first day on the job seemed like she was behind the wheel of a NASCAR vehicle without any driving experience. The job was so fast-paced that she didn't even feel herself moving. Her trainer, Megan, was patient and kind, but Mia knew she was getting on Megan's nerves. Mia had so many questions and ignorance about law and the justice system. She didn't even know the twenty-seven amendments, let alone clients' rights and labor laws. Mia didn't consider herself to be religious.

She didn't affiliate or identify with any religious group. She just knew that there was a Divine Creator who favored her and sometimes talked to her, and she was happy with that. She wasn't a churchgoer, Bible-thumper, scripture reciter, or cross-wearing woman. She didn't know the difference between Methodists and Baptists, Muslims, and Christians, or praising and worshiping. She just knew of the Divine Creator. But lately, that wasn't enough.

She didn't want to know of the Divine Creator; she wanted to know the Divine Creator. Saturday night, she told Lydia that they would be waking up early Sunday morning to go to church. Lydia whined, "Aww, Mom!

I already have to wake up early Monday, Tuesday, Wednesday, Thursday, and Friday for school. Now, I have to go to bed early on Saturday to wake up early on Sunday. Then I'll have to go to bed early Sunday to wake up early Monday. I need a break!" Mia took a deep breath. She had to remind herself that Lydia was just a kid being a kid. And it was her fault that Lydia wasn't used to going to church. In a calm demeanor, Mia said, "Other children will be there. And we get to sign you up for summer camp with a lot of other kids tomorrow, too." "Other kids will be there?" Lydia's eyes beamed. "Yep." Mia nodded. "Okayyyy. I'll go to sleep." Mia wasn't used to waking up early on a Sunday, either.

Back home, Sundays were for football and sleeping in before going into her late shift at work. *I guess I'll have to pencil church in on Sundays, every now and again,* Mia thought to herself. Mia and Lydia were twenty minutes late to church. She beat herself up about it until The Voice said to her, *"It's better than not going at all. From this point on, make me a priority, and your timing will fall into place."*

When Mia pulled into the church's parking lot, there were parking-lot greeters and door greeters. Everyone greeted her with a smile and/or handshake. She felt so welcomed, and Lydia was loving all the attention. They hadn't missed much of the service. The choir was still singing when they walked in. Lydia loved music, so the praise and worship songs really caught her attention.

When the music was over, Mia was shocked to see who stood in the pulpit to deliver the sermon: Attorney Johnson. She was in such a rush to make it inside the church that she didn't pay attention to whose name was on the marquee. Even if she had, it wouldn't have clicked in her mind. Never in a million years would she have thought that he was also a preacher. He was too meek, gentle, mild, and nice. Weren't pastors boisterous, arrogant, loud, flashy, attention-seeking, high and mighty, and thought they were above and better than everyone? None of that described Attorney Johnson—none of it.

The title of his sermon was, "Don't wait until you die to meet the Divine Creator." He preached from Psalms 63:1. Attorney Johnson, well, Minister Johnson, began, "Psalm 63:1 begins with, 'O Divine Creator, thou art my Creator; early will I seek thee…' Saints, this means, get up! Wake Up! Open your eyes! You have slept long enough. Seek Him while it's early before it gets to be too late."

Minister Johnson continued with his sermon, but one thing alone stuck with Mia: *Wake up!* She definitely had slept long enough. It was time to open her eyes and spend time with the Divine Creator. It was time for her daughter to see her spending time with the Divine Creator. It was time for Mia and Lydia to awaken from their slumber, get off of autopilot, and get to know the Divine Creator.

When Pastor Johnson extended the invitation for people to come to the front and join the church or request prayer, Mia's legs flew from underneath her, and she instinctively took Lydia with her. "Church, let's welcome Ms. Ramos and her daughter, Lydia." The church clapped and yelled out, "Welcome!" "Thank you for visiting us today.

Why did you come up to the front of the church, Ms. Ramos?" "I don't want to just visit the Divine Creator. I want to dwell with Him," Mia answered. "Whoa," Pastor Johnson exhaled. "Yes, Ma'am. Psalms 91:1 says that whoever *dwells* in the shelter of the Divine Creator will find rest in Him. It doesn't say whoever visits Him. Ms. Ramos, you are definitely on the right path. What brought about this change?" "I'm awake now."

Two weeks later, little Lydia watched her mom get baptized. Up until that point, the highlight of Mia's life was graduating high school. She never thought anything could top that moment of walking across the stage and going home to so many gifts waiting for her in the living room. But on this day, she was born again and received the gift of eternal life.

THE VOICE: MISHAWN CHILDERS

Nothing, for sure, would top this. Being baptized wasn't the only thing that made her be born again or that saved her from her sins; being baptized also solidified her stance and belief.

Dallas introduced her to many lifelong Christian friends—lifelong Christian friends whom she didn't hesitate leaving her little girl with, lifelong Christian friends whom she didn't mind confiding in, and lifelong Christian friends whom she could pop in on without a phone call or text and just laugh. These friends encouraged her and supported her, without end.

Because of their love and support, Mia finally graduated college. After over seven years of pursuing a college education on and off since the age of eighteen, she received her four-year degree.

Mia felt guilty, at times, for being so blessed and favored by the Divine Creator. She looked around at her family and noticed they were still struggling. They were still living just to work and working just to live. She questioned the Divine Creator why He didn't do the same thing for them that He did for her. He told her that He warned her family and talked to her family just like He warned Mia and talked to Mia.

The difference was that Mia listened and took heed; her family didn't. Her family was the reason for their downfall and shortcomings. They ignored The Voice, time and time again. But Mia didn't ignore it, and that made all the difference. While in her final year of college, she began dating a classmate named Daniel. Daniel had no children and loved Lydia as if she were his own—and so did his family. Everything about Daniel was warm, welcoming, and inviting.

Daniel was a man Mia could rest in. He was a breath of fresh air. Mia had no idea that men like Daniel existed. She waited around for him to change and for his true colors to show. But day after day, situation after situation, time after time, Daniel remained the same loving man he always was.

The Voice told Mia that Daniel was her husband, and she believed Him. After a little over a year of dating, Daniel and Mia married. Within five years of marriage, they brought forth into the world three beautiful kids together. Lydia finally had her siblings that she was always begging her mother for, and Lydia treated them like the answered prayers that they were.

Two years into their marriage, Daniel became a politician, and Mia was able to quit her job. Mia went from a lifetime of working just to be able to go back to work to spend all day taking care of her home and children. She also started investing.

Once upon a time, being able to pay all her bills was the only goal she had, and at the time, that was unattainable and unreachable. Now, her goal was to be able to make it to all of her kids' games and recitals without the other children feeling left out. She had a family. She became a Proverbs-31 woman. She lived instead of existing. She thrived instead of surviving. And it was all because she listened to The Voice.

THE VOICE: MISHAWN CHILDERS

Conclusion: As the Voice Guides You...

I have walked through the pain, the doubt, and the moments where I ignored the signs. I know what it's like to feel stuck, to wonder if things will ever change. But I also know the power of listening, of surrendering to God's voice, and stepping into our blessings.

Self-love taught me that I am enough. I no longer compare myself to others or let my past define me. When I embraced who I was in God's eyes, I found peace, confidence, and the ability to move forward without fear.

Missed blessings are no longer my story. I choose to listen. I choose to trust. When God whispers, I answer. And in that obedience, I have found doors opening, opportunities arising, and a path that is clear, even in the unknown.

Hard times will come, and enemies may rise, but they no longer have power over me. I now recognize the people meant to walk with me and those I must let go of. God's voice has guided me to healthy relationships, purposeful connections, and unwavering faith.

There were moments when I felt I had lost everything, but what I didn't realize was that God was clearing the way for something greater. Each trial was preparing me, shaping me into the person I was meant to be. Looking back, I now see that the struggles were not punishments but stepping stones to my transformation.

Healing doesn't happen overnight, but it does happen when we trust the process. As I started walking in alignment with His plan, I saw the power of faith in action. I stopped settling for less and started living with intention and purpose.

I stand firm in my faith, trusting that each step I take is part of a greater journey. The voice that once seemed distant is now my daily guide, leading me toward a future filled with hope, joy, and fulfillment. As you finish this book, I hope you choose to listen, trust, and move forward. Let God's voice be your guide, and you will never be lost again.

THE VOICE: MISHAWN CHILDERS

The Voice Oath

From this day forward, I shall hear.
I will pray always, and keep you near.

No longer can I stray from Your Will.
Instead, I choose to listen and be still.

I submit fully to you, as my guide,
Knowing you will never leave my side.

To You, I place my life in your hands.
On this truth, I fully stand.

Listening, to make the wisest choice.
Here I am, the Divine Creator; I will follow *The Voice*.

THE VOICE: MISHAWN CHILDERS

Trust Your Inner Guide to Discover the Wisdom Within: A Workbook to Assist You

Congratulations on taking the next step in your journey of spiritual growth and personal transformation! The rest of this book from this point forward comprises a workbook designed to complement the stories in *The Voice* by offering you practical tools, reflection exercises, and action steps that will help you cultivate a deeper understanding of how to tune in to the voice of the Divine Creator, also known as the Holy Spirit. Whether you're new to recognizing this voice or looking to strengthen your ability to discern and act on it, this workbook is for you.

In *The Voice*, we explored stories of people who faced life's most pivotal moments, either by heeding or ignoring that inner guidance. Now, this workbook is your opportunity to reflect on your own experiences and apply these lessons to your daily life. Just as each story showed the consequences of following or ignoring the voice, this workbook will lead you through a process of recognizing the moments when the Holy Spirit is speaking to you—and how you can make more empowered decisions by listening to that divine guidance.

The Importance of This Journey: Learning to Listen, Recognize, and Act on the Voice of the Divine Creator

Listening to the voice of the Divine Creator is one of the most important spiritual disciplines you can develop. It's more than just a skill—it's a transformational practice that impacts every aspect of your life. The voice of the Divine Creator is always present, but too often, the noise of everyday life can drown it out. Through intentional practice, we can learn to quiet the distractions, recognize that still, small voice, and act on what we hear. This is the journey we'll be taking together.

When you learn to listen to the Holy Spirit, you open yourself up to the wisdom and direction that can guide you through life's challenges, uncertainties, and opportunities. Recognizing this voice will help you align your actions with the Divine Creator's plan for your life, giving you peace in your decisions, clarity in your purpose, and confidence to step into your future. This workbook is designed to help you do just that—to build your sensitivity to the voice of the Divine Creator and strengthen your ability to act in faith.

What to Expect from this Workbook: A Guide to Reflection, Practical Steps, and Action Plans

This workbook is structured to be a hands-on companion to *The Voice*. It will guide you through a series of personal reflections, practical exercises, and action plans to deepen your connection to the Holy Spirit. Here's what you can expect as you work through each section:

1. Personal Reflection: Each section begins with thought-provoking questions and journaling prompts designed to help you reflect on your own experiences. You'll be invited to examine past moments when you may have heard the voice of the Divine Creator, whether you followed it, and what the outcome was. These reflections will help you gain insight into your patterns and create a foundation for change.

2. Practical Steps: Following each reflection, you'll find actionable steps to help you consistently hear and act on the voice of the Divine Creator. These steps are simple but powerful tools for cultivating awareness and creating space for the Holy Spirit to guide you. Whether it's setting aside quiet time, eliminating distractions, or developing new habits of listening, these practical exercises will equip you to integrate spiritual guidance into your everyday life.

3. Action Plans: This workbook will not only help you listen and reflect but also take action. You'll create personalized action plans to implement what you've learned, so you can turn spiritual insights into a real-life transformation. You'll be encouraged to take concrete steps—whether big or small—toward living in alignment with the Divine Creator's voice and plan for your life.

As you work through the steps, remember that this is a process. Some days, you may feel more connected to the Holy Spirit, and other days, the noise of life may seem overwhelming. Be patient with yourself. The key is consistency and a willingness to trust that the Divine

THE VOICE: MISHAWN CHILDERS

Creator is always speaking, even when we don't hear Him immediately. Through this journey, you'll learn not only to recognize His voice but to trust it and live by it. By the end of this workbook, you'll have a stronger understanding of how the Holy Spirit speaks to you, and how to move forward in life with faith, courage, and clarity. This is a sacred journey, and I'm excited to walk it with you. Let's get started!

THE VOICE: MISHAWN CHILDERS

The Voice is Your Superpower but How Do You Know It's His Voice?

Imagine having a superpower that gives you clarity when things get chaotic, protects you from harm, aligns with your purpose, strengthens your confidence, and is always available.

That's exactly what the voice of the Divine Creator—the Holy Spirit—is. It's your divine superpower, constantly guiding you toward the life you're meant to live. Let's break down the key ways the voice acts as your superpower:

1. Clarity during Chaos
In moments of confusion or when the noise of life is overwhelming, the Holy Spirit brings clarity. When things feel uncertain, listening to the voice helps you discern the right path and navigate challenges with wisdom.

Reflection:
- Think of a time when you felt lost or overwhelmed. What happened when you quieted your mind and sought clarity from the Divine Creator?

- How did that clarity help you see things differently? Write about it.

Action Step:
- Spend 5 minutes each day in quiet reflection or prayer, asking the Holy Spirit to give you clarity in any current areas of confusion. Write down the insights you receive.

2. Protection from Harm
The voice of the Divine Creator is always looking out for you, guiding you away from danger—whether that's a harmful relationship, a bad decision, or even physical danger. When you follow the voice, you're protected in ways you may not always understand at the moment but will see later.

Reflection:
• Recall a time when you had a "gut feeling" or an internal nudge that kept you from making a bad choice. How did that experience unfold?

• Write about how you've experienced protection from the Holy Spirit's guidance in your life.

Action Step:
• When you feel uneasy or sense a warning, pause and pray for discernment. Write down what you feel the voice is telling you, and choose to follow it, even if it's uncomfortable.

3. Alignment with Your Purpose

The Holy Spirit always aligns with your higher purpose. When you tune in, you'll find that the guidance you receive directs you toward your calling and the life the Divine Creator has designed for you. This alignment brings peace and a deep sense of fulfillment.

Reflection:
• When have you felt most aligned with your purpose? What role did the voice of the Divine Creator play in leading you to that place?

• Write down any recent moments when you felt disconnected from your purpose and consider how tuning into the voice could guide you back.

Action Step:
• Set a weekly intention to ask the Holy Spirit to reveal how your current actions align with your greater purpose. Reflect on any adjustments you need to make to stay on course.

4. Strengthening Your Confidence

Listening to the voice gives you a profound sense of confidence. When you know the Holy Spirit is guiding you, doubts fade, and your ability to make bold, faith-filled decisions grows. This confidence isn't based on your strength, but on trusting the power of divine guidance.

Reflection:
• Write about a time when following the voice gave you the confidence to make a tough decision. How did it feel to act in faith, knowing you were being led by the Divine Creator?

• Consider areas of your life where you're currently struggling with self-doubt. How can the voice of the Divine Creator help you find confidence in those areas?

Action Step:
• Each time you're faced with self-doubt, pause and remind yourself that the voice is your superpower. Write down one affirmation that reinforces your trust in the Holy Spirit's guidance, such as, "I am confident because I am divinely led."

5. Always Available
The voice of the Divine Creator isn't something you have to earn or search far and wide to find. It's always available to you. Whether you're facing a major life decision or simply looking for peace in your everyday life, the Holy Spirit is with you, ready to guide and support you.

Reflection:
• Have you ever gone through a season where you didn't feel like the Divine Creator's voice was available to you? Reflect on that time and how it impacted your decisions and mindset.

• Write about how knowing that the Divine Creator's voice is always available brings you comfort today.

Action Step:
• Develop a habit of checking in with the Holy Spirit throughout your day. Start small—set reminders on your phone to pause for a moment of stillness and ask, "What are you guiding me to today?" Keep a journal to note how your awareness of the voice grows over time.

THE VOICE: MISHAWN CHILDERS

Embrace Your Superpower

Your ability to hear and act on the voice of the Divine Creator is your greatest superpower. It empowers you to navigate life's challenges with clarity, protection, purpose, confidence, and assurance that divine guidance is always within reach. Use this workbook to strengthen that connection, and remember—you are never alone. ***The Holy Spirit*** is always with you, speaking life and truth into your journey.

Navigating Confusion: When Your Feelings Conflict with the Voice of the Divine Creator

There will be times when your emotions, thoughts, and desires seem to compete with the voice of the Divine Creator. You may feel uncertain about whether you're truly hearing the Holy Spirit or whether you're being influenced by fear, ego, or outside pressures. In those moments, it's important to develop the discernment to recognize which voice is guiding you.

The Holy Spirit speaks in a calm, consistent manner, often leading you toward decisions that align with your higher purpose, even if they're difficult or uncomfortable. Yet, emotions like fear, anxiety, and ego-driven desires can create confusion and push you in directions that may feel immediately satisfying but are not aligned with the Divine Creator's plan. Learning to distinguish between these conflicting voices is essential for spiritual growth and for making decisions that reflect your true calling.

Action Steps for Navigating Confusion:

1. Gut vs. Ego: Recognizing the Divine Creator's Intuition vs. Emotion-Led Decisions

When you're in the midst of confusion, it's important to understand the difference between a decision led by the Holy Spirit and one driven by fear or ego. The voice of the Divine Creator, or your intuition guided by the Holy Spirit, often brings peace—even if the decision is difficult. In contrast, decisions influenced by ego or fear are often hasty, fueled by anxiety, and focused on short-term satisfaction.

Reflection:
• Reflect on recent situations where you faced conflicting feelings. Write down the emotions that came up (e.g.: fear, pride, impatience).

• Now, think about how the voice of the Divine Creator might have been speaking during that time. Were there moments of calmness or inner nudges that pointed you in a different direction?

- How can you tell the difference between your gut instinct (Holy Spirit-led intuition) and emotions fueled by fear or ego? Write down your thoughts.

Action Steps:
- Create a "check-in" routine for when you're faced with a major decision or feel conflicted. This could include pausing to ask, "Is this decision motivated by fear, pride, or insecurity, or is it driven by peace and trust in the Divine Creator's guidance?"

- Write down a situation this week where you felt torn between your gut instinct and your emotions. Identify which feelings were based on fear or ego, and which were aligned with deeper peace.

2. Seek Clarity: Ways to Cut through Confusion

In times of confusion, it's crucial to take intentional steps to seek clarity. While emotions may be swirling, clarity often comes when we stop, ask for guidance, and wait for a response. The Holy Spirit may guide you in subtle ways, through inner peace, through the words of a trusted friend, or even through circumstances aligning to confirm a direction. Here are some ways to seek clarity when conflicting feelings arise:

I. Use Prayer and Stillness: When emotions are running high, take time to pause and pray. Ask the Holy Spirit to reveal the right path to you and to help you separate your ego-driven desires from His will. In the stillness, clarity often emerges.

- **Reflection:** Think of a time when prayer or stillness helped you gain clarity. How did the Holy Spirit guide you in that moment? Write about the experience.

II. Ask for Signs: Sometimes, we need a little extra confirmation. Don't be afraid to ask for a sign or a "nudge" from the Divine Creator. It could come in various forms—through scripture, a conversation with a friend, or even a small coincidence that points you in the right direction. The key is to be open and attentive to how the Divine Creator communicates.

- **Reflection:** Have you ever asked for a sign and received one that helped clarify a decision? Write about how it unfolded and how it gave you peace in your choice.

III. Seek Wise Counsel: When you're struggling to discern the Divine Creator's voice, wise counsel from trusted spiritual mentors or friends can help you gain perspective. Sometimes, others can see what we can't. A fresh perspective, especially from someone grounded in faith, can help confirm whether you're following the right path.

- **Reflection:** Write about someone in your life who has given you wise counsel in the past. How did their guidance help you find clarity? Who can you go to now when you're feeling confused?

Action Plan:

• Weekly Practice: When confusion arises, choose two methods from the list above (prayer, signs, or counsel) to practice consistently. For instance, start your mornings with a short prayer asking for clarity in any area where you feel stuck. Keep a journal of any signs or confirmations you receive throughout the week, and reflect on how they help you make decisions.

• Accountability Partner: Identify someone you trust who can be a sounding board when you're feeling conflicted. This person can help you discern between what is ego-driven and what feels aligned with the Divine Creator's voice.

By practicing these steps, you'll begin to fine-tune your ability to separate conflicting emotions from the voice of the Divine Creator. Over time, recognizing the Holy Spirit's guidance will become clearer, and your trust in that voice will strengthen, even in times of confusion.

THE VOICE: MISHAWN CHILDERS

The Importance of Acting on the Voice

Why Action Matters:

Hearing the voice of the Divine Creator is an incredible gift, but the true power lies in acting on what you hear. The Holy Spirit guides you toward your purpose and protects you from harm, but that guidance is only effective when it's followed by action. It's in your response to the Divine Creator's voice where transformation happens—whether in your relationships, career, or personal growth.

When you act on the voice, you're exercising faith. It's an act of trust in the Divine Creator, even when you don't fully understand the outcome. By stepping out in obedience, you invite the Holy Spirit to work in your life, unlocking blessings, growth, and a deeper spiritual understanding. On the other hand, hesitation or ignoring the voice can result in missed opportunities, delays, and prolonged struggles.

Why is action so critical?

Because faith without action is incomplete. When you act on the Divine Creator's voice, you align yourself with His will and purpose for your life. In fact, some of the greatest blessings often come from moments of obedience when you choose to act despite fear, uncertainty, or doubt.

Reflection Activities:

1. Journal Prompt: Think back to a time when you acted on a feeling or intuition that you knew came from the Divine Creator. Maybe it was a decision to end a toxic relationship, pursue a new job, or help someone in need. Write about that experience:

- **What led you to act?** Was there a specific moment or feeling that confirmed you were being guided by the Holy Spirit?

- **What was the outcome?** How did things unfold once you took action? Did you experience peace, a breakthrough, or unexpected blessings as a result?

- **How did this experience impact your faith?** Did it strengthen your trust in the Divine Creator's voice? Write down any lasting effects that moment had on your relationship with the Divine Creator.

By reflecting on past moments of obedience, you'll see how acting on the voice creates ripples of positive change in your life.

2. Goal-Setting:

The Divine Creator's voice often leads us to take steps, big or small, toward fulfilling our purpose. This week, challenge yourself to act on something you feel the Holy Spirit leading you to do. It could be as simple as offering a word of encouragement, starting a project that's been in your heart, or spending more time in prayer.

- Choose one small step that you will take this week to act on the voice. Write it down and set a timeline for when you'll follow through.

- After completing the action, journal about how you feel afterward. Did taking that step bring you more clarity, peace, or a sense of purpose? Did it challenge your faith?

Overcoming Doubt When You Are Unsure:

Doubt is a natural part of the human experience, especially when it comes to discerning the voice of the Divine Creator. You might wonder if you're really hearing from the Holy Spirit or if it's just your thoughts or desires getting in the way. You may question whether you're strong enough, ready enough, or worthy enough to take the steps you're being led to.

It's normal to feel unsure when following the Divine Creator's guidance, particularly when the path isn't clear or seems risky. However, overcoming doubt is the key to growing in faith and allowing the Divine Creator to work in your life. Doubt doesn't mean you're off-course; it simply means you're being stretched. The key is to push past it, reminding yourself that the Divine Creator's voice is trustworthy and His plans are always for your good.

Doubt often arises because we fear failure, judgment, or the unknown. But remember, the Holy Spirit never leads you astray. The Divine Creator's voice is filled with wisdom, love, and protection, and even when things don't make immediate sense, His plan is always perfect.

Action Steps:

1. Faith over Fear: Scripture is one of the most powerful tools for overcoming doubt. It reminds you of the Divine Creator's promises and His unshakable faithfulness. When you're feeling unsure about following the voice, lean on the truth of the Divine Creator's word to strengthen your faith. Here are three scriptures to affirm your trust in the Divine Creator's guidance:

• **Proverbs 3:5-6** – "Trust in the Divine Creator with all your heart and lean not on your understanding; in all your ways submit to Him, and He will make your paths straight."

• **Isaiah 30:21** – "Whether you turn to the right or to the left, your ears will hear a voice behind you, saying, 'This is the way; walk in it.'"

• **Jeremiah 29:11** – "For I know the plans I have for you," declares the Divine Creator, "plans to prosper you and not to harm you, plans to give you hope and a future."

Reflection Activity:
Write down these scriptures (or others that resonate with you) in a journal. When doubt arises, take a few moments to read them aloud and reflect on the Divine Creator's promises. How does this strengthen your confidence in hearing and following His voice?

2. Affirmations: In moments of doubt, developing positive affirmations rooted in faith can help quiet the noise of uncertainty. Affirmations are powerful reminders of the Divine Creator's presence and guidance, and they help redirect your focus from fear to trust. Here are a few examples to inspire your affirmations:

- "I trust that the Divine Creator's voice is leading me on the right path, even when I cannot see the full picture."

- "I am divinely guided by the Holy Spirit, and I have the courage to act on that guidance with confidence."

- "The Divine Creator's plans for my life are good, and I will follow His voice, knowing that I am protected and loved."

Action Steps:
Create two or three affirmations that resonate with you and write them down. Keep them in a place where you'll see them often—whether on your phone, on your bathroom mirror, or in a notebook. Repeat these affirmations when doubt creeps in to reinforce your faith and trust in the Divine Creator's voice.

By practicing these steps, you'll not only deepen your trust in the Divine Creator's voice but also equip yourself to overcome the natural doubts that arise along the way. As you continue to act on what you hear, your confidence will grow, and you'll see the fruits of following divine guidance more clearly in your life.

Personal Guide to Hearing the Voice of the Divine Creator

1. Daily Quiet Time

☐ Set aside a time each day to quiet your mind (e.g.: 15 minutes in the morning).

☐ Begin with prayer or meditation to ask the Divine Creator for clarity.

☐ Take deep breaths, and listen without distractions.

2. Scripture Reflection

☐ Reflect on a daily verse that encourages stillness and faith (e.g.: Psalm 46:10).

☐ Keep a journal of scripture passages that resonate with you.

3. Listen for Confirmation

☐ Pay attention to external confirmations (e.g.: advice from trusted sources, repeated signs).

☐ Look for alignment between what you sense and what scripture or spiritual mentors say.

4. Act on the Voice

☐ Write down what you sense the Holy Spirit is saying.

☐ List one actionable step you will take, based on what you hear.

☐ Track the results of following that action.

5. Stay Consistent

☐ Commit to listening to the voice daily, even when making small decisions.

☐ Eliminate distractions, such as overconsumption of media, that pulls you away from the voice.

THE VOICE: MISHAWN CHILDERS

Final Reflection and Commitment

As you come to the end of this workbook, take a moment to pause and reflect on everything you've learned about the voice of the Divine Creator—the Holy Spirit—and the importance of listening, trusting, and acting on that divine guidance. This journey isn't just about gaining knowledge; it's about transformation—allowing yourself to grow in faith, deepening your spiritual awareness, and fully embracing the life the Divine Creator has for you.

The Divine Creator's voice is constantly speaking, gently guiding you toward His plans and purpose for your life. He speaks through moments of stillness, during your daily routines, and even in times of chaos. The Holy Spirit is your trusted companion, always available, always loving, and always desiring to lead you on a path of peace, joy, and fulfillment. But this guidance is only impactful when you choose to listen and take action.

Reflection Questions:

1. What have I learned through this process?

Take a few moments to think about your journey through this workbook. What new insights have you gained about hearing and responding to the voice of the Divine Creator? Has your understanding of intuition, faith, and spiritual guidance deepened? Write down some of your key takeaways.

2. How have I experienced the Divine Creator's voice in the past?

Look back on your life and recall moments when you knew the Divine Creator was speaking to you—whether through a prompting in your spirit, a scripture that came alive, or a person speaking words that confirmed what you already felt. How did you respond? How did it impact your life? Reflect on how these moments shaped your faith journey.

3. What's stopping me from fully trusting the voice of the Divine Creator?

We all have barriers that can get in the way of fully trusting and acting on the Divine Creator's guidance. Whether it's fear, doubt, or a desire for control, acknowledging these barriers is the first step toward overcoming them. Write down any obstacles that may have kept you from following the Holy Spirit's voice in the past.

Commitment to Trust and Act on the Voice:

Now that you've completed this workbook, it's time to make a commitment—a decision—to consistently tune in, trust, and act on the voice of the Divine Creator in your life.

1. I commit to making space for the voice.

In the busyness of life, it's easy to overlook those moments when the Divine Creator is trying to speak to you. Set an intention to create space for stillness and reflection in your daily life, where you can intentionally listen to the Holy Spirit. Whether it's through prayer, meditation, or journaling, find time to be quiet before the Divine Creator and invite His voice into your heart.

2. I commit to recognizing the voice.

You've learned to distinguish between the voice of the Divine Creator and competing thoughts led by fear or ego. Moving forward, commit to paying attention to those divine nudges, the inner peace, and moments of clarity that come from the Holy Spirit. Be mindful of how the Divine Creator speaks to you in different ways—through scripture, circumstances, people, or even your intuition.

3. I commit to acting on the voice.

Hearing the voice of the Divine Creator is only the first step. Trusting and acting on it is where true transformation happens. Challenge yourself to act with courage when you feel led by the Holy Spirit. Even when the path isn't clear, step forward in faith, knowing that the Divine Creator's plans for you are good. Write down one specific action you will take this week, based on something you feel the Divine Creator is calling you to do.

4. I commit to overcoming doubt.
Doubt is a natural part of following the Divine Creator's guidance, but you don't have to let it hold you back. When feelings of uncertainty or fear arise, remind yourself of the Divine Creator's faithfulness and His promises. You've equipped yourself with tools—scripture, affirmations, and faith-building practices—to overcome doubt. Commit to using these tools to strengthen your trust in the Divine Creator's voice when challenges come.

Final Prayer of Commitment:

Heavenly Father,
I thank You for the gift of Your Holy Spirit, who guides me, speaks to me, and leads me into all truth. I acknowledge that I cannot walk this journey of faith alone, and I am grateful for Your constant presence in my life. As I move forward from this workbook, I commit to tuning in more closely to Your voice. Help me to recognize when You are speaking and give me the courage to act on Your guidance. Strengthen my faith when doubt arises and remind me that Your plans for me are always good. I trust You, Divine Creator, and I surrender my path to you. May Your voice always be the loudest in my life.

Action Steps for the Journey Ahead:

- **Continue journaling:** Keep a regular practice of writing down what you sense the Holy Spirit is speaking to you. This helps you track your progress and reflect on how the Divine Creator's guidance is unfolding in your life.

- **Stay accountable:** Share your journey with a trusted friend, mentor, or spiritual guide. Having someone to discuss your experiences with can offer encouragement and help you stay committed to acting on the voice of the Divine Creator.

- **Celebrate your growth:** Take time to celebrate the moments when you follow the Divine Creator's voice and see the results in your life.

These moments are worth acknowledging and will strengthen your confidence in hearing and trusting the Holy Spirit.

Final Exercise:

Write down three key lessons you've learned through this workbook and how you will continue to apply them to your life. Commit to spending time each week tuning into the voice and asking the Divine Creator for guidance in the journey ahead.

A Note from the Author

Thank you for reading! Please leave a review wherever book reviews are accepted.

About The Author

Mishawn Childers

Mishawn Childers is the author of **Discover You!** *6 Steps to Achieving Purpose*, as well as a professional speaker who was trained by Les Brown via **Zig Ziglar Inc.** She is also a certified life coach.

Mishawn is a wife to James and a mother of four. Mishawn's goal is to help people realize that their greatest potential is achieved when they listen to and obey the voice of the Divine Creator. She hopes the stories in this book will encourage and inspire the reader to walk in faith and listen to his voice.

Let's Stay Connected & Keep Growing

Your journey doesn't stop here—**God's voice is still speaking!** I would love to continue walking alongside you as you step boldly into your purpose and destiny. Here's how you can stay connected:

📧 Let's Stay in Touch

- **Website:** https://mishawnchilders.com
- **Email:** mishawnnchilders@gmail.com
- **LinkedIn:** https://www.linkedin.com/in/mishawn-childers-82351416b/

🎥 Free Training – Grab Your Free Automated Webinar!

Want to dive deeper? Sign up for my **free automated webinar** on **Hearing God's Voice & Walking in Your Purpose.** It's packed with wisdom, action steps, and inspiration to help you go further.

➡ **Access it here:** mishawnnchilders@gmail.com

📺 Follow Me on YouTube

Get weekly faith-filled insights, mindset shifts, and encouragement to **help you silence doubt and step into your destiny.**

🎬 **Subscribe here:** http://YouTube.com/@mishawnchilders

Ready for More? Let's Talk!

If you're reading this and thinking, **"Wow, I want more! I need clarity on what God is saying to me,"** then let's connect for a **20-minute 'Hearing God's Voice' Call.**
In this call, we'll dive into:
- What's keeping you stuck
- How to hear God's direction for your next step
- Ways to move forward in confidence

Schedule your call here: mishawnnchilders@gmail.com

You were **made for more.** God has called you for a purpose. **This is your time.** Let's step into it together!

www.ingramcontent.com/pod-product-compliance
Lightning Source LLC
Chambersburg PA
CBHW071457160426
43195CB00013B/2152